BIG BOOK

of Bible Story Coloring Activities

David C Cook®

transforming lives together

www.davidccook.com

BIG BOOK OF BIBLE STORY COLORING ACTIVITIES FOR EARLY CHILDHOOD
Published by David C Cook
4050 Lee Vance Drive
Colorado Springs, CO 80918 U.S.A.

David C Cook U.K., Kingsway Communications
Eastbourne, East Sussex BN23 6NT, England

ISBN 978-0-8307-7248-3

© 2018 David C Cook

The content included in this book was originally published in *Bible Stories to Color & Tell Ages
3–6* by Standard Publishing in 2005 © Standard Publishing, ISBN 978-0-7847-1770-0.

Cover Design: James Hershberger
Illustrator: Daniel A. Grossmann

Printed in the United States of America

1 2 3 4 5 6 7 8 9 10

082717

Contents

New Testament

Introduction

Big Book of Bible Story Coloring Activities for Early Childhood includes Bible story pictures and related activities children can complete that correlate to favorite Bible stories of preschool, pre-K, and kindergarten children.

Coloring Pictures

Coloring pictures provide a quick and easy way to introduce a Bible story. These coloring pages will help young children develop fine-motor skills as they color and will allow them to experiment with working toward a finished piece. While a simple coloring picture is fun for many children, consider making it part of a more active learning experience. Try one of these creative ideas for using coloring pictures as a teaching tool to encourage more active learning for kids:

- **Touch and Feel Pictures**—Provide rice, beans, cotton, glitter, fabric, felt, or popcorn for children to attach to their coloring pages using glue.
- **Thematic Bulletin Boards**—Add specific coloring pictures based on a teaching theme to a bulletin board with an appropriate title.
- **Bible Lesson Visuals**—Enlarge a coloring picture that illustrates a story you are teaching. Use the picture to introduce or review a story.
- **Personal Coloring Books**—Copy 10 to 15 different coloring pages based on a theme you are teaching. Help children create their own coloring books using tape, yarn, or folders to keep the pages together.
- **Puzzles**—Mount a coloring picture on card stock and cut the page into puzzle pieces. Kids can work the puzzle as they review the Bible story.
- **Mosaic Pictures**—Have children glue small pieces of torn construction paper to a coloring picture rather than simply coloring the page.

- **Mail It Home**—Children love to get mail! Welcome a visitor or stay in touch with an absentee by mailing a coloring picture to a child's home address with a personal note to the child attached to the page.

Activity Pages

The activities in this book teach kids to retell the Bible stories in their own words using pictures that help them remember the order of important events. When children retell Bible stories in their own words, they remember them long after they leave the classroom.

Because the fine-motor skills are developing rapidly at this age level and can vary greatly, some activities in this book are designed to be simpler for younger children and some are more challenging for older children. The activities were specially designed so children can complete them with little assistance from the teacher and cutting patterns follow a simple design so children learning to cut will be successful!

Special Activity Instructions

Some of the activities in this book require a full page for the activity itself. For those activities you will be directed to this page for assembly directions.

Red Sea Pamphlet Instructions (p. 48)

Help children color and cut out the pamphlet around the outside edge (do not cut along the dotted lines). Children should color the back of the pamphlet blue to look like water. Lay the pamphlet in front of you with the picture facing up. Fold the right panel in on the dotted line so it covers the center panel. Fold the left panel in on the dotted line so it covers both the right and center panels. Children can open the left panel and then the right panel as they retell the story of God's people crossing the Red Sea.

Ten Men Finger Puppets Instructions (p. 200)

Help children color and cut out the ten finger puppets. Children can fold each puppet at the dotted line so each puppet has two sides. Tape the puppets to fit around the children's fingers (one per finger). Children can use the finger puppets to retell the story of Jesus healing ten men. They can show all ten puppets when they tell about the ten men asking Jesus to help them. They can turn their hands around to show the ten healed men when they tell about Jesus healing them. They can hold up just one puppet when they tell about one man coming back to thank Jesus.

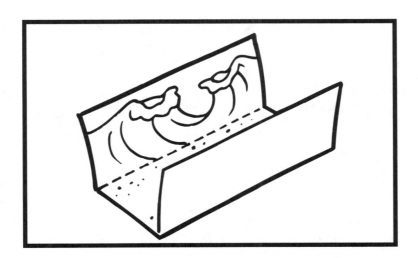

God Made the Sky and Earth

Creation Square

Supplies
- copy of the Creation Square (1 per child)
- crayons or washable markers
- scissors

Directions
Help children color each of the four scenes. Direct them to color scene 1 a light color above the dotted line and a dark color below the dotted line to show that God created light and dark. Help children cut out the square along the outside solid edge only (do not cut apart individual squares). Children can color the back of the square using their favorite colors.

Fold each smaller scene square along the dotted line so the pictures are folded inside. Children open each scene as they tell what God made on days one to four of creation.

Genesis 1

God Made the Sky and Earth

Big Book of Bible Story
Coloring Activities for Early Childhood
© David C Cook. Permission granted to photocopy for ministry purposes only.

God Made Fish and Birds

Fish and Birds Pop-Up Card

Supplies
- copy of the Fish and Birds Pop-up Card (1 per child)
- crayons or washable markers
- scissors
- glue (optional)
- construction paper (any color, optional)

Directions
Help children color the pop-up cards. Cut out the cards along the solid outside lines. Fold each card in half along the dotted line while folding the pop-up piece along the dotted lines. The pop-up piece should fold inside the card and will pop up when the card is opened. Children can use the cards to tell how God made fish and birds. Children can also count the fish and birds as a reminder that God made fish and birds on day five of creation.

Optional: Before folding the card, attach it to a piece of colored construction paper for a firm backing.

Thank You, God, for fish and birds.

Genesis 1

God Made Fish and Birds

God Made Animals

Animal Flip-Flap Book

Supplies
- copy of the Animals Flip-Flap Book and word pieces (1 per child; continued on p. 14)
- crayons or washable markers
- scissors
- construction paper (any color, 1 sheet per child)
- glue sticks

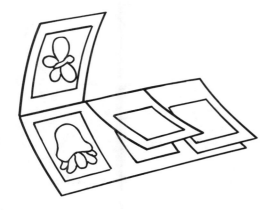

Directions
Help children color and cut out the animals and word pieces on the solid lines. Fold a piece of construction paper in half lengthwise. Cut the top flap of the paper into three equal sections stopping the cut at the fold line (each flap should be 4" wide; see the example). Glue the word pieces to the front of the flaps (one per flap so it reads "God Made Animals" when the flaps are closed). Lift the three flaps and glue the six animals inside the flaps (glue three to the inside top and three to the inside bottom; see the example). Children can use the flip-flap books to tell about the different animals God made. They can count the animals (six total) as a reminder that God made animals on the day six of creation.

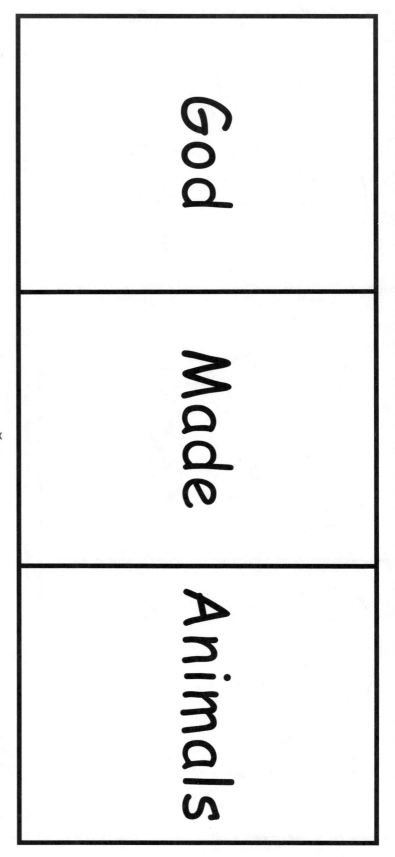

Genesis 1

God Made Animals

Big Book of Bible Story
Coloring Activities for Early Childhood
© David C Cook. Permission granted to photocopy for ministry purposes only.

Genesis 1
God Made Animals

God Made a World for People

Creation Storybook

Supplies

- copy of the Creation Storybook cover (1 per child)
- copies of coloring pages 8, 10, 12, 15, 17 for each child
- crayons or washable markers
- scissors
- construction paper (any color, 7 sheets per child)
- glue sticks
- 3-hole punch
- yarn
  (any color)

Directions

Help children color and cut out the storybook cover on this page. (Children should cut freely around the crayon border.) Using the coloring pages listed, children can assemble a book showing all of the things God made. Attach the cover and each of the coloring pages to separate sheets of construction paper (any color). Use the last piece of construction paper as a back cover for each book. Punch holes down the sides of the books. Tie each book using yarn. Children can use their coloring books to tell about God making the earth, the fish and birds, the animals, and people.

Genesis 1

Big Book of Bible Story
Coloring Activities for Early Childhood
© David C Cook. Permission granted to photocopy for ministry purposes only.

God Made a World for People

God Made People

People Story Wheel

Supplies

- copy of the People Story Wheel and wheel cover (1 per child; continued on p. 19)
- crayons or washable markers
- scissors
- paper fasteners (1 per child)

Directions

Help children color and cut out the story wheel and cover. Punch a hole in the center of both the wheel and cover. Attach the cover over the wheel using a paper fastener. Children can rotate the cover and look through the opening as they retell the story of God making people. Kids can tell God made a man and a woman, He put them in charge of the animals, and He gave people and animals food from plants to eat.

Genesis 1
God Made People

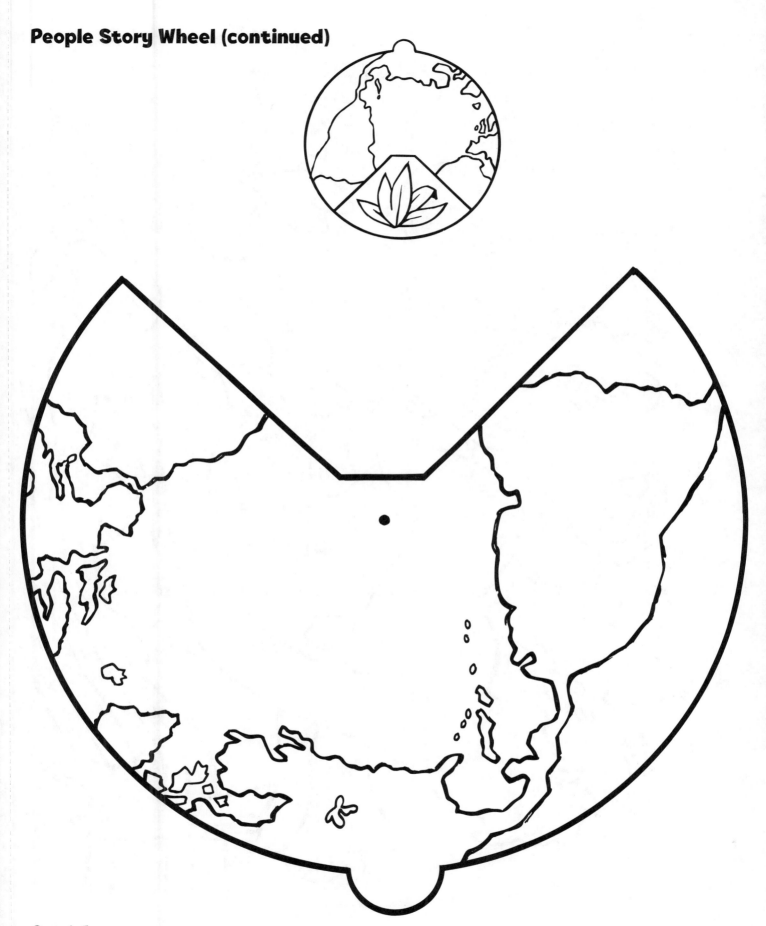

Genesis 1
God Made People

God Made Adam and Eve

Adam and Eve Booklet

Supplies

- copy of the Adam and Eve Booklet pages (1 per child; continued on p. 22)
- crayons or washable markers
- scissors
- construction paper (1 sheet per child)
- glue sticks

Directions

Color and cut out the pictures of Adam and Eve doing various things as well as the individual sentences. Fold a piece of construction paper in half widthwise and then in half again to make a small book (see the example). Attach the words "God Made Adam and Eve" to the front of the booklet. Attach the pictures and their matching word strips to the remaining three pages of the booklet (attach the word strips below the pictures). Children can use the booklets to tell that God made people special with hands, arms, and legs. As children tell about each part God made, encourage them to share what they like to use their hands, arms, and legs for.

God Made Adam and Eve

God made hands.

© David C Cook. Permission granted to photocopy for ministry purposes only.

God made arms.   God made legs.

Genesis 1–2
God Made Adam and Eve

God Made My Senses

Five Senses Flash Cards

Supplies

- copy of the Five Senses Flash Cards (1 per child; continued on p. 25)
- crayons or washable markers
- scissors
- white card stock (optional)

Directions

Help children color the pictures on the flash cards. Then help them cut apart each set of cards on the solid lines and fold along the dotted lines so a picture of a body part is on one side and a picture depicting what you use that body part for is on the other side (for example, the mouth on the back of the apple, the nose on the back of the flower, etc.). Children can use the cards to tell about the five senses God gave to people and how we use them.

Optional: Copy the cards on white card stock to make the cards sturdier.

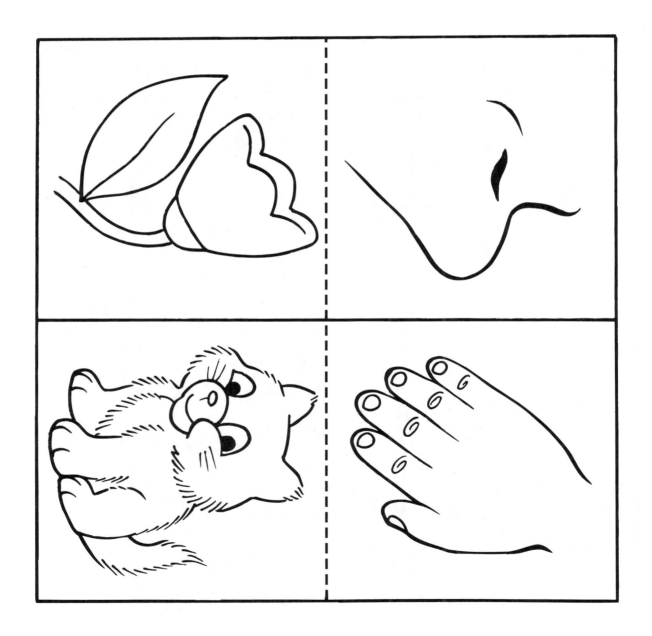

Genesis 1–2; Proverbs 20

God Made My Senses

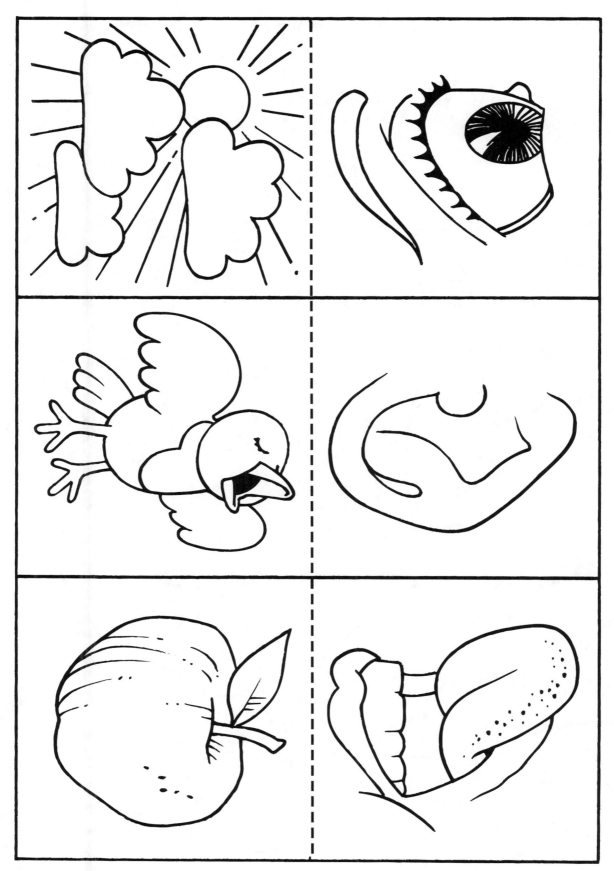

Genesis 1–2; Proverbs 20

God Made My Senses

Big Book of Bible Story
Coloring Activities for Early Childhood
© David C Cook. Permission granted to photocopy for ministry purposes only.

God Made Me Special

Fill-In a Face

Supplies

- copies of the Fill-In a Face and facial features (1 per child; continued on p. 28)
- crayons or washable markers in various skin tones as well as other general colors
- scissors
- glue sticks
- yarn and tape or glue *(optional)*

Directions

Help children color the faces using skin tone crayons they feel match their own skin colors. Allow children to use other colors to add hair and eyebrows that also match their own. Help children cut out a set of ears and a nose that resembles their own and attach them to their faces in the appropriate places. Children can finish by adding additional features such as freckles to their faces to make them look more like themselves. Kids can use the Fill-In a Face activity to tell about how God made each person special.

Optional: Use various colors of yarn for the hair and allow kids to choose their own colors and attach the yarn to their face activities.

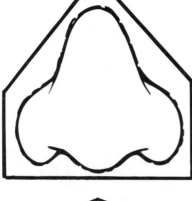

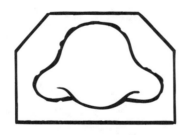
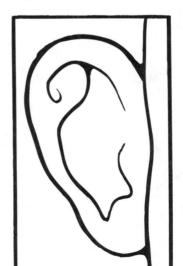
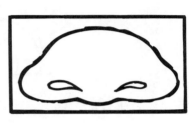
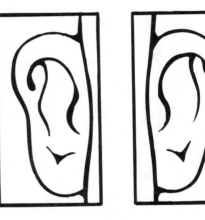
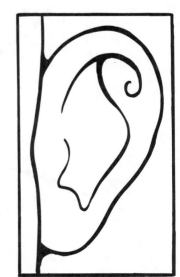
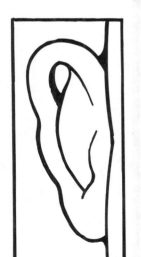

Genesis 1–2; Psalms 8, 139; Matthew 10

God Made Me Special

Genesis 1–2; Psalm 8, 139; Matthew 10
God Made Me Special

Noah Builds a Boat

Floating Ark Puppet

Supplies

- copy of the Floating Ark Puppet (1 per child)
- crayons or washable markers
- scissors
- glue sticks
- jumbo craft sticks (1 per child)
- blue construction paper (½ sheet per child)
- glue sticks
- yarn and tape or glue (optional)

Directions

Help children color and cut out the ark puppet (cut around the solid outline, do not cut on the dotted line). Fold the ark on the dotted line so the two sides are back-to-back. Glue the ark around the edges and glue a craft stick to the inside bottom of the ark (between the two halves), forming a two-sided stick puppet. Cut a long slit lengthwise in the center of the construction paper. Insert the ark puppet through the slit (see the example). Children can show the ark floating and tell about Noah building the ark, Noah, his family, and the animals getting into the ark, and the flood causing the ark to float.

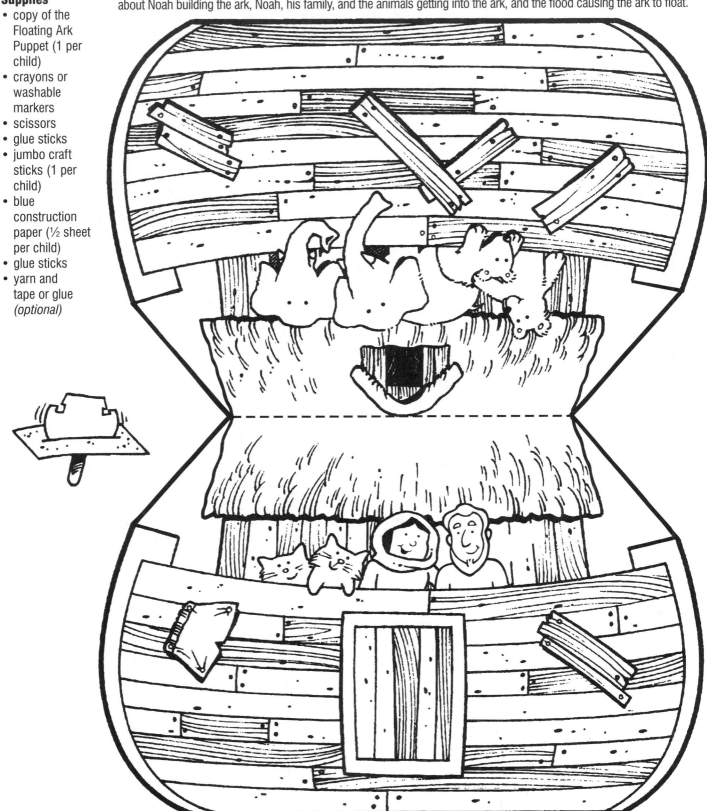

Genesis 6–7

Noah Builds a Boat

Noah and the Flood

Animal Memory Game

Supplies

- 2 copies of the Animal Memory Game cards for each child
- crayons or washable markers

Directions

Help children color the animal cards. They should color each pair of animals to look alike. Help children cut out the cards. Use the cards to play a game of memory. Children should turn all of the cards so they are facedown on the floor or a table in front of them. They should begin by turning over one card and then trying to find its match. If they find a match they may keep the pair of cards. If they do not find a match they should turn over both cards and try again. Kids can use the pairs of animals as a reminder that the animals boarded the ark in pairs and they came off of the ark with Noah after the flood.

Genesis 7–9

Noah and the Flood

Abram Moves

Story Case

Supplies

- copy of the Story Case and scenes (1 per child)
- crayons or washable markers
- scissors
- paper lunch bags (1 per child)
- glue sticks

Directions

Help children color and cut out the Story Case covers and the scenes. Attach the covers to the paper lunch bags (see the example). Place the scenes inside the bags. Children can use the Story Cases to tell the story of Abram's move:

1) Abram packed up his family and his home (show the tent).
2) Abram and his family traveled a long way (show the camel).
3) Abram built altars to the Lord along the way to worship and thank God (show the stone altar).

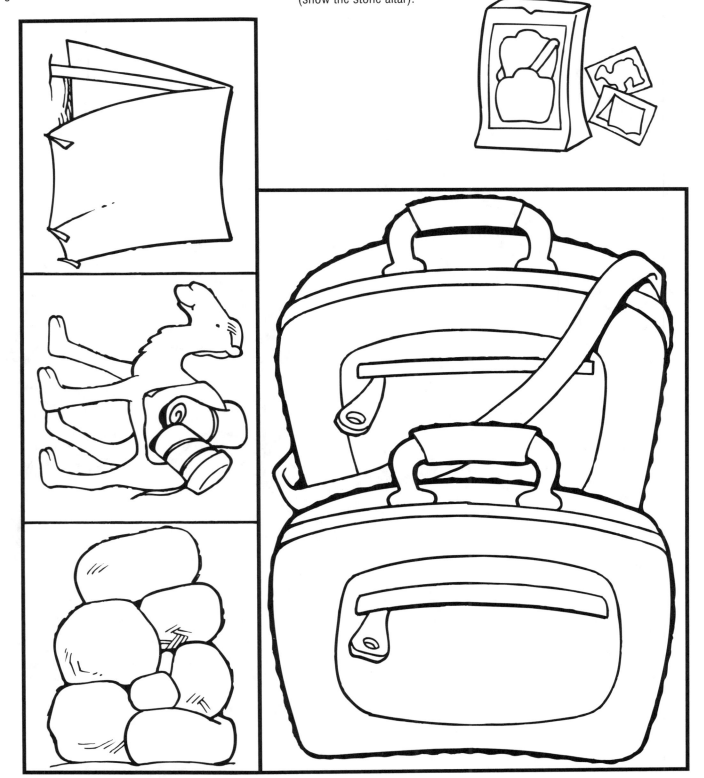

Genesis 12

Abram Moves

Abram and Lot

Abram and Lot Finger Leg Puppets

Supplies

- copy of the Abram and Lot Finger Leg puppets (1 per child; preferably on card stock)
- crayons or washable markers
- scissors

Directions

Before class, cut out the puppets and holes (or at least the holes). Help children color and cut out the puppets. Cut out the holes in the open circles where the legs should be. Children can place their fingers through the open holes and make the puppets walk. Children can use the puppets to retell the story of Abram and Lot choosing their land. Lot should walk first to show that Abram let Lot choose first.

Optional: Copy the puppets on white card stock to make them sturdier.

Abram

Lot

Genesis 13

Abram and Lot

Abraham and Sarah Have a Baby

Family Photo Album

Supplies

- copy of the Family Photo Album (1 per child)
- crayons or washable markers
- scissors

Directions

Help children color the pictures in the album. On scene 3, children should draw in the faces for how they think Abraham and Sarah felt when God gave them a son. Help children cut out the album along the outside border (do not cut on the dotted lines). Fold the album in half lengthwise along the long dotted line. Fold the album in half again along the dotted line so the long family photo is folded inside. Scene 1 should be the front; scene 3 should be the back. Children can use the albums to tell about Abraham and Sarah having a baby:

1) Abraham and Sarah were very old.
2) God gave Abraham and Sarah a son.
3) Abraham and Sarah were very happy when Isaac was born.

Genesis 17—18, 21

Big Book of Bible Story
Coloring Activities for Early Childhood
© David C Cook. Permission granted to photocopy for ministry purposes only.

Abraham and Sarah Have a Baby

Joseph as a Boy

Joseph Puppet

Supplies

- copy of the Joseph Puppet (1 per child)
- crayons or washable markers
- scissors
- craft sticks (1 per child)
- glue sticks
- arge foam cups
- gray or brown paint *(optional)*
- small sponges *(optional)*

Directions

Help children color both sides of the Joseph Puppet and cut it out along the outside solid edge (do not cut on the dotted line). Fold the Joseph puppet on the dotted line so the two sides are back to back. Attach the puppet to a craft stick by gluing the stick inside the bottom of one side, and then glue the two sides together. Children can turn the puppet as they use it to retell the story of Joseph as a boy:

1) Joseph was a shepherd (show the plain side).
2) Joseph's father made him a colorful coat (show the coat side).
3) Joseph's brothers sold Joseph as a slave and took away his coat (show the plain side).

Optional: Cut a slit in the bottom of a foam cup. Allow kids to color or sponge paint the cup gray or brown to resemble the well where Joseph was thrown. Kids can insert the stick of the Joseph puppet into the slit and raise Joseph in and out of the well as they retell the story.

Genesis 37, 39

Big Book of Bible Story
Coloring Activities for Early Childhood
© David C Cook. Permission granted to photocopy for ministry purposes only.

Joseph as a Boy

Joseph Serves God All His Life

Pyramid of Service

Supplies

- copy of the Pyramid of Service (1 per child; preferably on card stock)
- crayons or washable markers
- scissors
- tape

Directions

Help children color the three scenes. Cut out the pyramid around the outside edge only (do not cut on the dotted lines). Fold the scenes along the dotted lines to form a triangle with the scenes showing on the outside. Tape the tab on scene 3 to the back of scene 1 so the pyramid stands on its own. Children can use the pyramids to retell the story of Joseph serving God:

1) Joseph served Potiphar in Egypt by taking care of everything Potiphar owned.
2) God was with Joseph when Joseph was chosen to help the king understand a dream.
3) Joseph's brothers came to Egypt and Joseph gave them the food they needed.

Genesis 39, 41–42, 45, 47

Joseph Serves God All His Life

Big Book of Bible Story
Coloring Activities for Early Childhood
© David C Cook. Permission granted to photocopy for ministry purposes only.

Moses Is Born

Baby Basket

Supplies

- copy of the Baby Basket (1 per child)
- brown construction paper (1 sheet per child)
- crayons or washable markers
- scissors
- glue

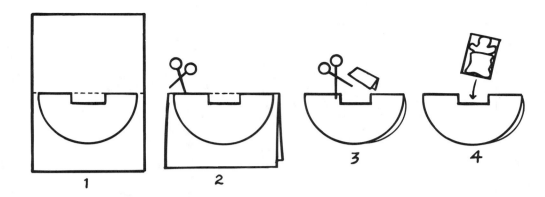

Directions

Help children color and cut out baby Moses and the basket. Glue the basket to a piece of brown construction paper (see illustration 1). Fold the construction paper in half along the top edge of the basket (see illustration 2). Cut around the curve of the basket, cutting through both halves of construction paper (do not cut along the top of the basket—leave the top edge folded). With the paper still folded in half at the top, cut along the rectangle shape in the top of the basket to create an opening (cut through both sides of the construction paper when cutting along this line; see illustration 3). The basket should rock side to side when placed on a table or other flat surface and tipped slightly. Children can insert baby Moses into the opening of the basket as they retell the story of Moses' birth (see illustration 4):

1) Moses' mother placed Moses in a basket (drop Moses through the opening in the basket).
2) Pharaoh's daughter found Moses (lift the front of the basket to pick up Moses and pull him out of the basket).

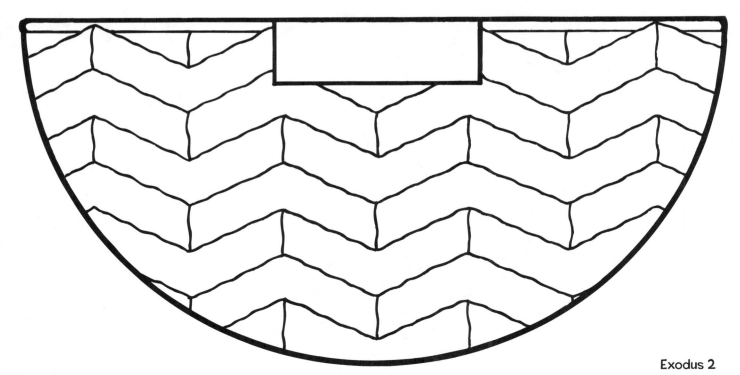

Exodus 2

Moses Is Born

Moses Leads God's People

Moses Spinner Game

Supplies

- copy of the Moses Spinner Game on card stock or mounted on cardboard (1 per child)
- crayons or washable markers
- scissors
- paper clips (1 per child)
- paper fasteners (1 per child)

Directions

Help children color the four scenes and cut out the square as one piece (do not cut between scenes). Attach a spinner in the center of the circle using a paper fastener and paper clip (loose enough for the paper clip to spin freely). Children can spin the paper clip. When the paper clip lands on a scene, kids can tell about that scene and how Moses led God's people:

1) From a burning bush God called Moses.
2) Moses was chosen to lead God's people.
3) God guided His people by a pillar of cloud during the day.
4) God guided His people by a pillar of fire during the night.

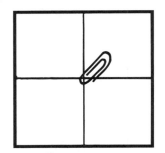

Exodus 3, 7–13

Moses Leads God's People

God's People Cross the Red Sea

Red Sea Pamphlet

See page 7 for supplies and directions for this activity

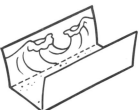

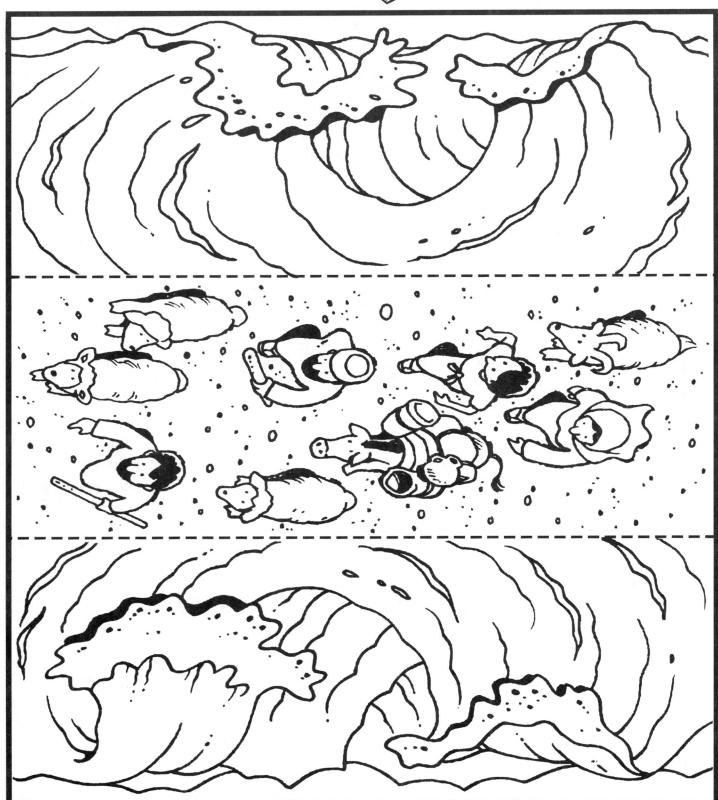

Exodus 13–15

God's People Cross the Red Sea

God Provides for His People

God Provides Flip-Flap Book

Supplies
- copy of the Flip-Flap Book (1 per child)
- crayons or washable markers
- scissors
- construction paper (any color, 1 sheet per child)
- glue sticks

Directions

Help children color and cut out the four scenes. Fold a piece of construction paper in half lengthwise. Cut the top flap of the paper into four equal sections, stopping the cut at the fold line (each flap should be 3" wide). Lift the flaps and glue the scenes under the flaps according to the numbers in the lower right corner of each scene. See the small image for an example. Children can use the flip-flap books to retell the story of how God provided for His people:

1) The people were hungry.
2) God sent manna and quail to feed His people.
3) The people were thirsty.
4) God provided water from a rock for His people.

Exodus 16–17

God Provides for His People

God Gives Ten Rules

Commandments Puzzle

Supplies

- copy of the Commandments Puzzle (1 per child; preferably on white card stock)
- crayons or washable markers
- scissors

Directions

Help children color the scenes in each puzzle piece and cut out the puzzle pieces individually. Children can assemble the puzzle and use it to tell about how God gave ten rules to His people.

1) God wanted His people to obey Him.
2) God called Moses up on a mountain.
3) God gave ten rules to Moses on stone tablets.
4) Moses brought the rules back down the mountain to the people.

Exodus 19–20, 24, 32

God Gives Ten Rules

Joshua and Caleb

Spy Matching Game

Supplies

- copy of the Spy Matching Game (1 per child)
- crayons or washable markers
- scissors

Directions

Help children color the scenes and cut out each scene along the solid lines so each child has eight separate scenes. Children should mix up the scenes and try to match each picture to its opposite to reveal what the spies were to look for in the land they were exploring.

1) Were the people in the land strong or weak?
2) Was the soil good or bad?
3) Were the cities surrounded with walls or not?
4) Were there trees or no trees?

Numbers 13–14

Joshua and Caleb

God's People Cross the Jordan River

Jordan Crossing Card

Supplies

- copy of the Jordan Crossing Card (1 per child)
- crayons or washable markers
- scissors

Directions

Help children color and cut out the cards on the outer line. Fold each card back along the long dotted line so the scenes are back-to-back. Fold the card in half again along the short dotted line so the people crossing the river are folded inside the card. Children can use the cards to retell the story of God's people crossing the Jordan River:

1) The Jordan River was flowing but God promised to part it for His people to cross.
2) God parted the river and the people walked through on dry land.
3) The people built an altar to God using 12 stones they collected from the dry river floor (children can count the stones in the altar) as a reminder of what God did that day.

Joshua 1, 3—4

Big Book of Bible Story
Coloring Activities for Early Childhood
© David C Cook. Permission granted to photocopy for ministry purposes only.

God's People Cross the Jordan River

The Fall of Jericho

Jericho Trumpets

Supplies

- copy of the Jericho Trumpets (1 per child)
- crayons or washable markers
- scissors
- tape

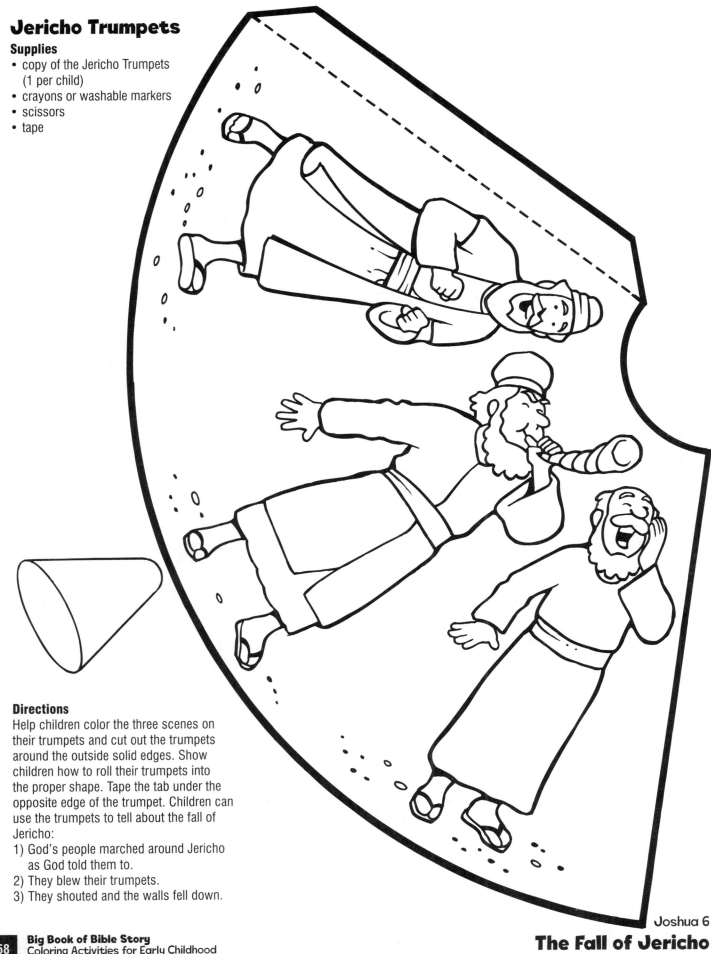

Directions

Help children color the three scenes on their trumpets and cut out the trumpets around the outside solid edges. Show children how to roll their trumpets into the proper shape. Tape the tab under the opposite edge of the trumpet. Children can use the trumpets to tell about the fall of Jericho:

1) God's people marched around Jericho as God told them to.
2) They blew their trumpets.
3) They shouted and the walls fell down.

Joshua 6
The Fall of Jericho

Joshua Talks to God's People

Big Book of Bible Story
Coloring Activities for Early Childhood

59

© David C Cook. Permission granted to photocopy for ministry purposes only.

Joshua Mask

Supplies

- copy of the Joshua Mask (1 per child)
- crayons or washable markers
- scissors
- jumbo craft sticks (1 per child)
- tape

Directions

Help children color and cut out the mask of Joshua. Cut out a place for the eyes and the mouth as indicated on the mask. Help children tape a craft stick to the back of the mask at the chin area. Children can hold the mask in front of their faces as they pretend to be Joshua talking to God's people. They can ask each other (as "Joshua") to choose if they will serve God just like Joshua asked the people.

Joshua 24

Joshua Talks to God's People

Gideon Leads God's Army

Gideon's Shield

Supplies

- copy of Gideon's Shield (1 per child)
- crayons or washable markers
- scissors
- brown construction paper *(optional)*
- glue sticks, tape *(optional)*

Directions

Help children color and cut out their shields as one piece. Children can use the shields to retell the story of Gideon leading God's army:

1) God wanted Gideon to lead an army.
2) God helped Gideon choose which soldiers to take with him in battle.
3) Gideon took 300 soldiers to fight with him.
4) On Gideon's signal, the soldiers broke bowls, held torches, blew horns, and shouted. They won the battle with God's help.

Optional: Children can glue their shields to pieces of brown construction paper to make them sturdier. Use a precut strip of brown construction paper and tape a handle on the back of each shield.

Judges 6–7

Gideon Leads God's Army

Ruth Makes Good Choices

Ruth Story Puppets

Supplies

- copy of the Ruth Story Puppets (1 per child)
- crayons or washable markers
- scissors
- jumbo craft sticks (4 per child)
- tape

Directions

Help children color and cut out the puppets along the solid lines. Attach each puppet to a craft stick. Use the puppets to retell the story of Ruth:
1) Orpah left Naomi but Ruth stayed.
2) Ruth went to the fields to gather grain, and there she met Boaz.
3) Ruth brought back grain for herself and Naomi.

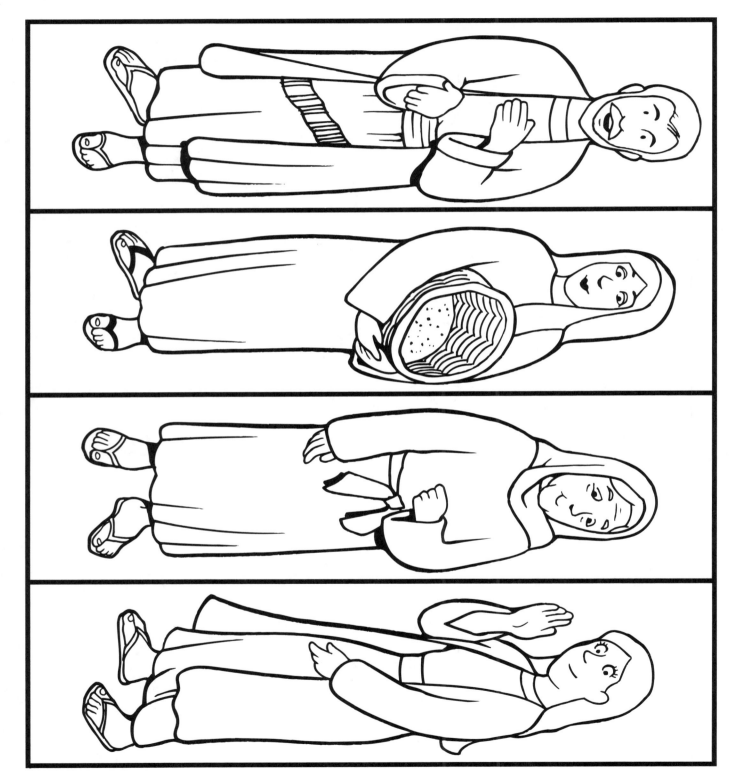

Big Book of Bible Story
Coloring Activities for Early Childhood

Ruth 1–2
Ruth Makes Good Choices

Samuel as a Boy

Samuel and Eli Hand Puppets

Supplies

- copy of the Samuel and Eli Hand Puppets (1 per child)
- crayons or washable markers
- scissors
- tape

Directions

Help children color and cut apart the puppets. Fold the two puppets in half on the dotted lines and tape the sides together so each puppet fits on a child's hand like a mitten. Help each child put the Samuel puppet on one hand and the Eli puppet on the other hand. Children can use the puppets to retell the story:

1) Samuel heard a voice calling his name (hold up Samuel).
2) Samuel went to Eli (hold up both Samuel and Eli and bring them together three times).
3) Samuel heard the voice again and he answered God as Eli had told him to (hold up Samuel).

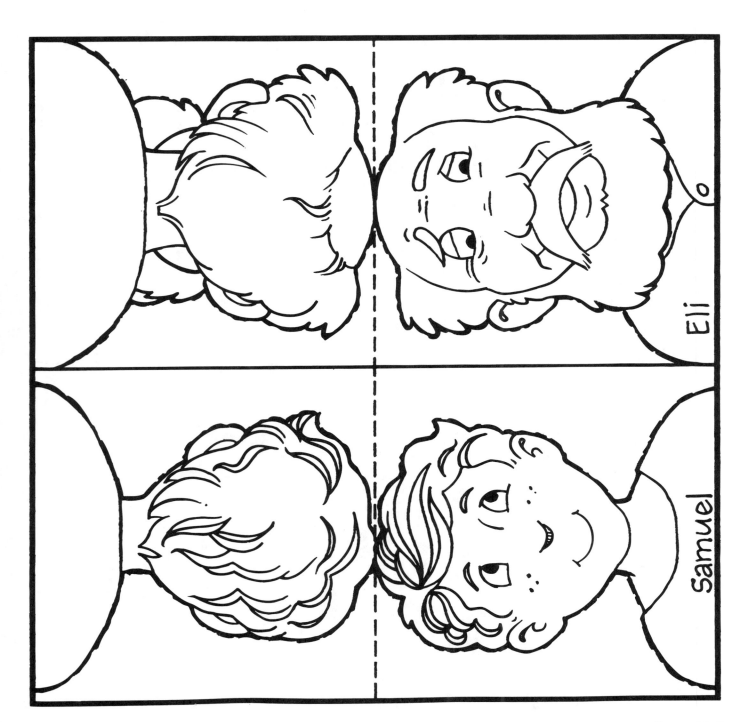

Samuel 1–3

Samuel as a Boy

Big Book of Bible Story
Coloring Activities for Early Childhood

Samuel Serves God All His Life

Scroll Mobile

Supplies

- copy of the Scroll Mobile (1 per child; continued on p. 69)
- crayons or washable markers
- scissors
- hole punch
- yarn or twine (any color)

Directions

Help children color and cut out the mobile pieces. Punch holes in each piece where indicated by the open circles. Tie each scroll to the closed scroll piece as shown in the example. Tie a piece of yarn to the center hole in the closed scroll piece and loop the yarn so children can hang their mobiles. Children can use the mobiles to retell the story of Samuel serving God all his life:

1) As a prophet, Samuel taught the people.
2) Samuel told the people who their king would be.
3) Samuel prayed for the people.

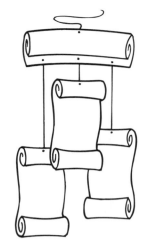

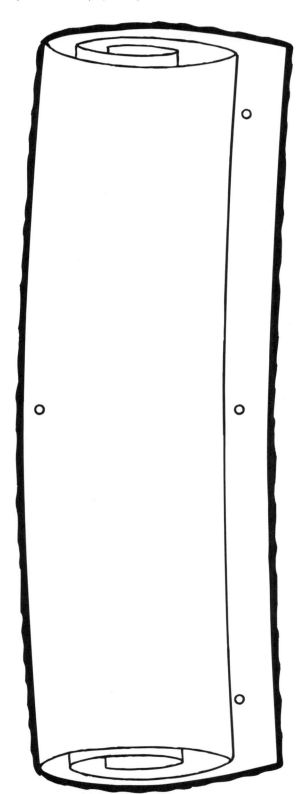

1 Samuel 3, 8–10, 12

Samuel Serves God All His Life

Scroll Mobile (continued)

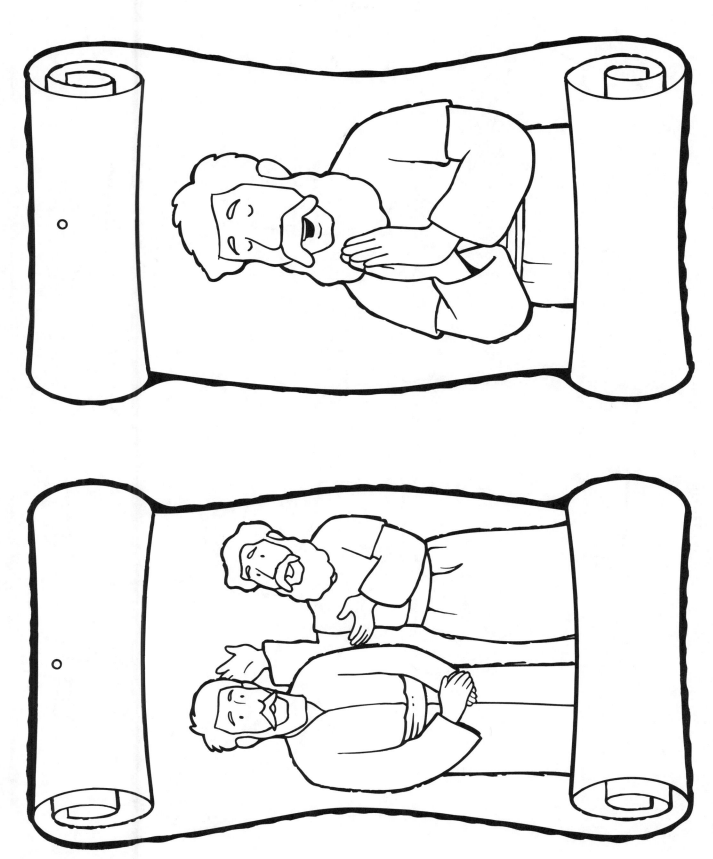

1 Samuel 3, 8–10, 12

Samuel Serves God All His Life

Big Book of Bible Story
Coloring Activities for Early Childhood
© David C Cook. Permission granted to photocopy for ministry purposes only.

David Plays for Saul

David's Harp

Supplies
- copy of the David's Harp booklet (1 per child; continued on p. 72)
- construction paper (any color, 1 sheet per child)
- crayons or washable markers
- scissors
- glue sticks
- 3" lengths of yarn (3 per child)
- tape

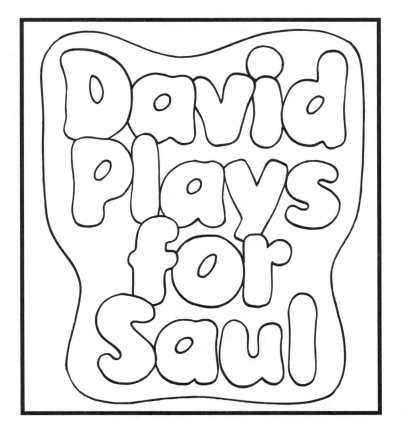

Directions
Prepare the booklets before class. Start by folding the construction paper in half lengthwise so that it is 12" long and 4½" high. Fold the construction paper again into three equal sections in alternating directions like an accordion (see the examples). Make one of these booklets for each child.

During class, help children color and cut out the four story pieces. Assist children as they glue the word piece to the front of their closed booklets (see step 1). Help children open the booklets and lay them flat on the table in front of them. Show children how to glue the picture of Saul on the first section, the picture of David on the middle section, and the harp outline to the last section (see step 2). Help children tape three pieces of yarn (each 3" long; any color) to the harp to make the strings. Kids can use the booklets to tell about David playing for Saul:
1) Saul was sad and did not feel well (show Saul).
2) David tended sheep and was called to come and play his harp for Saul (show David).
3) David played his harp and Saul felt better (show the harp).

David's Harp (continued)

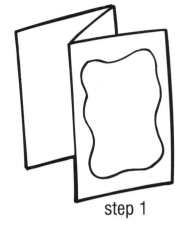

step 1

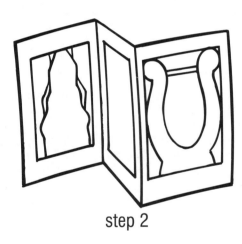

step 2

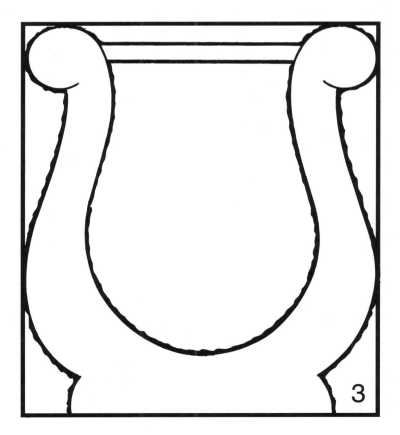

David Meets Goliath

David and Goliath Puppets

Supplies

- copy of the David and Goliath Puppets (1 per child)
- paper lunch bags (2 per child)
- crayons or washable markers
- scissors
- glue sticks

Directions

Help children color and cut out the David and Goliath Puppets by cutting around the outside edge and also through the mouth areas where indicated by the horizontal lines. Attach each puppet to a paper lunch bag as shown in the example (glue the top of the face above the fold and the bottom of the face below the fold so that the puppets' mouths open and close). Children can use the puppets to retell the story of David and Goliath from the perspective of either character. Encourage children to use their imaginations and tell about how David might have felt when Goliath teased him or what Goliath might have thought when he first saw David.

1 Samuel 17

David Meets Goliath

David and Jonathan

Window Scenes

Supplies

- copy of the Window Scenes (1 per child)
- construction paper (1 sheet of gray for every 6 children and 1 sheet of brown for every 9 children)
- crayons or washable markers
- scissors
- glue sticks

Directions

Before class, cut three rectangles out of construction paper for each child. Two of the rectangles should be 2½" by 3" (gray) and the third should be 3¼" by 3" (brown).

During class, help children color Jonathan's house gray and the three window scenes as they choose. Help children put glue on one long edge of each of the two gray rectangles and glue that edge to one side of each of the top two scenes so that the flap can be folded open to reveal the picture underneath (see the example). Have children repeat this with the brown piece over the bottom scene. Children can open the flaps to see and tell the story of David and Jonathan:

1) David lived at Jonathan's house (show the house).
2) David and Jonathan were good friends, and Jonathan gave some of his own things to David (open the top left flap).
3) The time came for David to leave Jonathan's house, and both friends were sad (open the top right flap).
4) David and Jonathan said good-bye and promised to be friends forever (open the door).

1 Samuel 18, 20

David and Jonathan

David and Mephibosheth

David's Kindness Doorknob

Hanger

Supplies •copy of the David's Kindness •Doorknob Ganger (1 per child)
• crayons or
  washable markers
• scissors
• glue

Directions
Help children color and cut out the two doorknob hangers. Children should glue them together so that the scenes are back-to-back. Children can place the hangers on doors in their homes to remind them of how David showed kindness in his home to Mephibosheth:

1) King David wanted to show kindness to Mephibosheth, so he invited Mephibosheth to always eat with him at his table.
2) David gave Mephibosheth the land that belonged to his family and, because Mephibosheth was crippled, David found men to work the land for him.

2 Samuel 9

David and Mephibosheth

Big Book of Bible Story
Coloring Activities for Early Childhood
© David C Cook. Permission granted to photocopy for ministry purposes only.

David Sings to God

David's Song Scroll

Supplies
- copy of David's Song Scroll (1 per child)
- crayons or washable markers
- scissors
- decorative ribbon or twine

Directions

Help children color and cut out the scrolls as one piece. Children can roll the scrolls and tie them with ribbon or twine. Children can unroll the scrolls as they tell about David singing to God:
1) David sang when he was happy.
2) David sang in the morning and at night.
3) David sang when he was afraid or needed help.
4) David sang and made music on instruments.

Help children think of ways and times they can sing to God too.

2 Samuel 22; Psalm 4–5, 23, 100, 122

David Sings to God

Big Book of Bible Story
Coloring Activities for Early Childhood

Solomon Prays to Know What Is Right

Crown Scenes

Supplies
- copy of the Crown Scenes (1 per child)
- 2" x 12" strips of construction paper (1 per child, any color)
- crayons or markers
- scissors
- tape

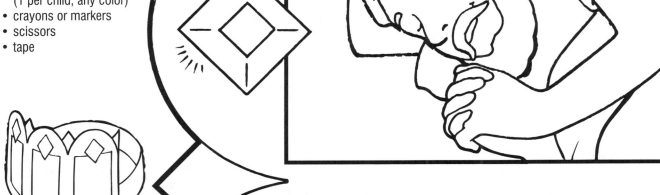

Directions
Help children color and cut out the crowns around the outside edges (do not cut apart individual scenes). Tape 2"-wide strips of construction paper to one side of the crowns and size them to fit the children's heads. Once the crowns have been sized, tape the other end of the strips of paper to the opposite sides of the crowns to make headpieces that can be worn (see the example). Children can wear the crowns as they pretend to be Solomon or use them to retell the story of Solomon praying to know what was right:

1) Solomon became king.
2) Solomon needed help knowing how to lead the people.
3) Solomon asked God to help him know right from wrong.

1 Kings 3—4

Big Book of Bible Story
Coloring Activities for Early Childhood

Solomon Prays to Know What Is Right

Solomon Builds the Temple

Unfolding Temple

Supplies

- copy of the Unfolding Temple story scenes square (1 per child; continued on p. 85)
- copy of the Unfolding Temple square (1 per child)
- crayons or washable markers
- scissors
- glue sticks

Directions

Help children color and cut out the square containing the four story scenes (do not cut apart the individual scenes; cut the square as one large piece). Help children color and cut apart the temple square by cutting along the solid lines (you should end up with four triangles that form the temple when assembled). Fold the square of four story scenes along the dotted lines so that the scenes are hidden inside when the flaps are folded down. Help children glue the four triangles of the temple over each of the folded flaps according to the numbers (piece 1 of the temple should be glued on top of the folded flap of scene 1, etc.). When the flaps are closed, the finished temple should be showing. As each flap is opened, a scene will appear. Children can use the Unfolding Temple to retell the story of Solomon building the temple:

1) Solomon wanted to build a special place to worship God.
2) Solomon had beautiful things made to put inside the temple.
3) Solomon prayed and asked God to watch over the temple.
4) The temple was finished.

1 Kings 5—8

Solomon Builds the Temple

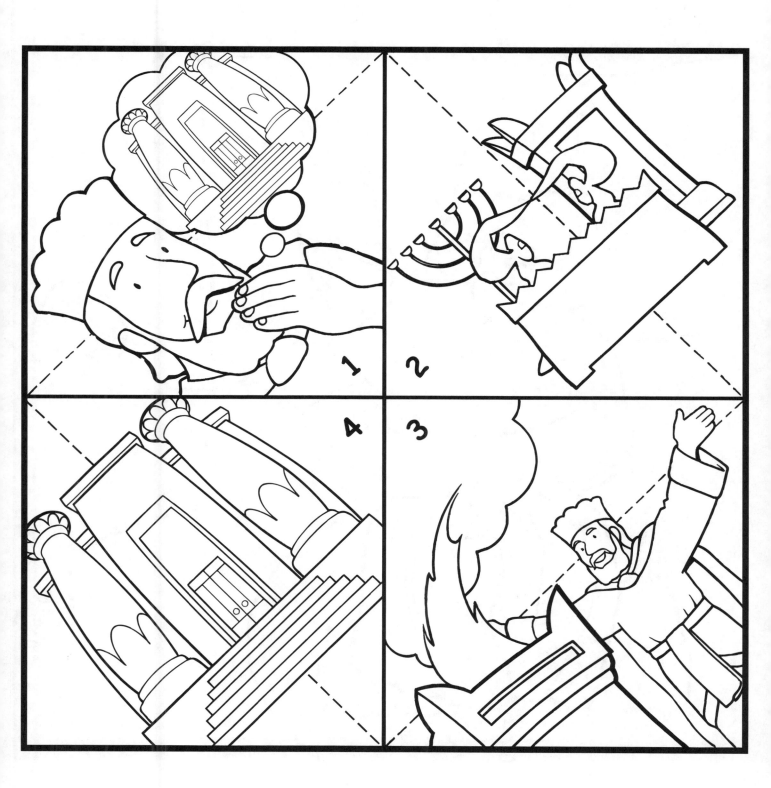

1 Kings 5—8

Solomon Builds the Temple

Big Book of Bible Story
Coloring Activities for Early Childhood
© David C Cook. Permission granted to photocopy for ministry purposes only.

Elijah Is Fed by Ravens

Ravine Picture Pocket

Supplies

- copy of the Ravine Picture Pocket scene and figures (1 per child; continued on p. 88)
- crayons or washable markers
- scissors
- tape
- construction paper (optional)

Directions

Help children color and cut out the ravine scene. Fold the bottom of the scene back along the dotted line and tape at each side to form a pocket behind the picture. Color and cut out Elijah and the ravens. Place Elijah and the ravens inside the pocket behind the picture. Children can use the ravine scene to retell the story of Elijah being fed by ravens.

1) God promised to give Elijah food and water during a drought.
2) Elijah drank from the brook (position Elijah to look like he's drinking from the brook).
3) God sent ravens to give bread to Elijah (show the raven holding bread flying toward Elijah).
4) God sent ravens to give meat to Elijah (show the raven holding meat flying toward Elijah).

Optional: You may want to attach the brook scene to a piece of construction paper prior to assembling the picture to make the picture sturdier.

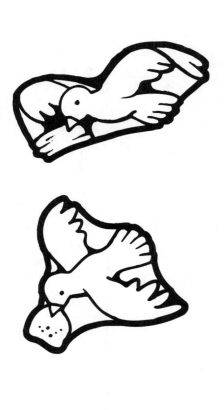

1 Kings 17

Elijah Is Fed by Ravens

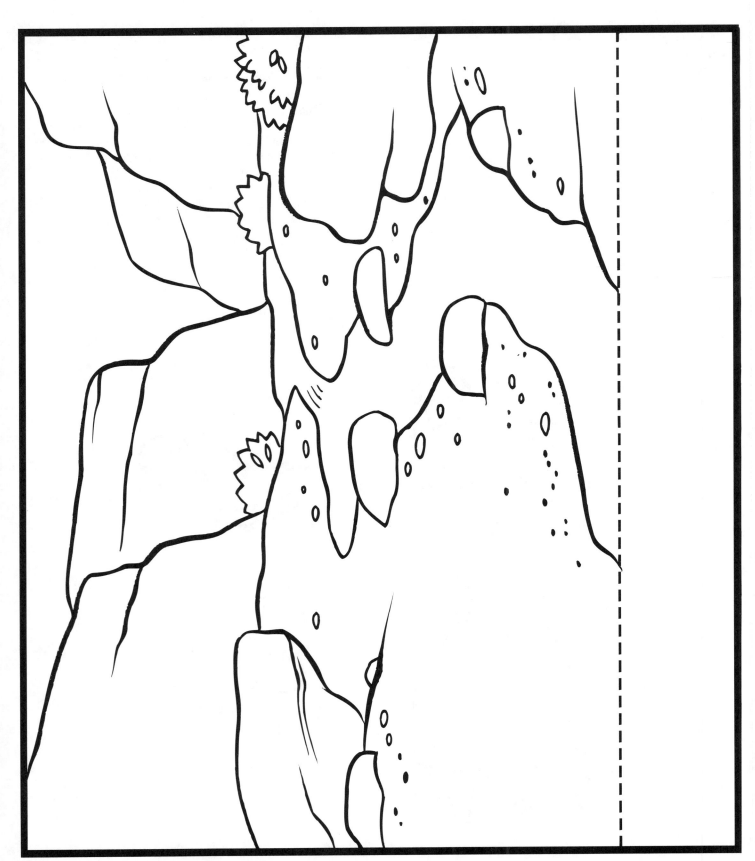

1 Kings 17

Elijah Is Fed by Ravens

Big Book of Bible Story
Coloring Activities for Early Childhood
© David C Cook. Permission granted to photocopy for ministry purposes only.

Elijah Helps a Widow

Widow's Jar

Supplies
- copy of the Widow's Jars (1 per child)
- crayons or washable markers
- scissors

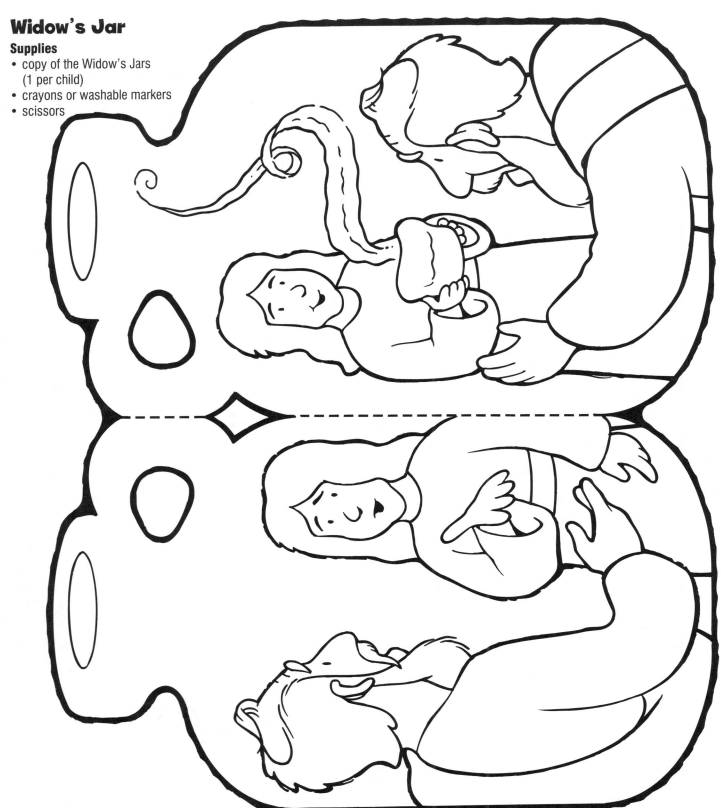

Directions

Help children color and cut out the two jars along the outside solid edge (do not cut along the dotted line). Color the back of the jars a solid color (to look like pottery). Color the scenes as desired. Children should fold the jars on the dotted line so that the scenes are folded inside like a book. Children can use the jars to retell the story of Elijah helping a widow:

1) Elijah asked a widow for bread but she did not have enough for him and for her family (show the first picture).
2) The widow obeyed and made the bread (show the second picture).
3) The widow's flour and oil did not run out—she always had enough (close the jars and pretend to pour oil over and over as you tell this part of the story).

1 Kings 17

Elijah Helps a Widow

Big Book of Bible Story
Coloring Activities for Early Childhood

Elijah Helps a Widow's Son

Big Book of Bible Story
Coloring Activities for Early Childhood

Celebration Banner

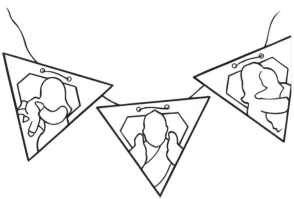

Supplies
- copy of the Celebration Banner (1 per child)
- crayons or washable markers
- scissors
- construction paper (various colors, 3 sheets per child)
- glue sticks
- hole punch
- yarn or twine

Directions
Celebrate with Elijah and the widow by making a colorful celebration banner! Help children color and cut out each triangle. Glue each triangle to a separate sheet of construction paper (various colors such as red, yellow, and blue). Cut around the triangle, leaving some of the construction paper showing on all sides of the triangle. Punch holes in each triangle where indicated by the open circles. String the banner together using yarn or twine as shown in the example. Children can hang the banners and use them to tell about Elijah helping a widow's son:
1) A widow's son was sick, and the widow was sad when her son died.
2) Elijah prayed for the boy.
3) God brought the widow's son back to life, and the widow was happy that Elijah helped her son.

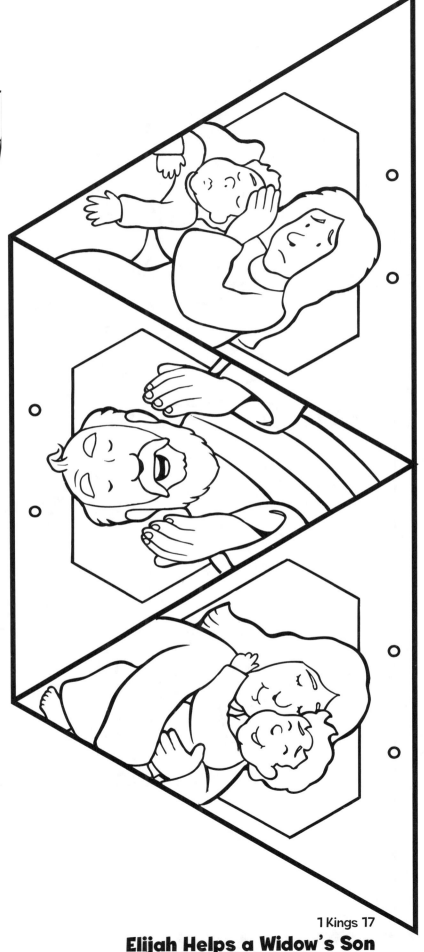

1 Kings 17

Elijah Helps a Widow's Son

Elijah and the Prophets of Baal

Fire from Heaven Card

Supplies

- copy of the Fire from Heaven Card (1 per child)
- crayons or washable markers
- scissors

Directions

Help children color and cut out the card around the outside edge. Cut along the solid line beside the fire scene, stopping when you reach the dotted line. Fold the card along the long dotted line so the fire scene and the scene showing a group of men standing are behind the three men and altar scenes. Fold the card along the remaining dotted line so the scene showing the five men is on the front and the fire piece is on the back of the card. Children can use the card to tell about Elijah and the prophets of Baal:

1) Elijah challenged more than 400 prophets of Baal to a contest.
2) The prophets of Baal danced and shouted trying to get Baal to send fire on their altar.
3) Elijah prayed to God to show that He is the one true God.
4) God sent fire from Heaven on Elijah's altar and the people believed in God (fold up the fire piece so that it appears above the altar—see the example).

1 Kings 18

Elijah and the Prophets of Baal

Elisha and a Widow's Oil

Jar Collage Penny Toss

Supplies

- copy of the Jar Collage Penny Toss scenes (1 for per child; continued on p. 97)
- construction paper (any color, 1 sheet per child)
- crayons or washable markers
- scissors
- glue sticks
- pennies (1 per child)

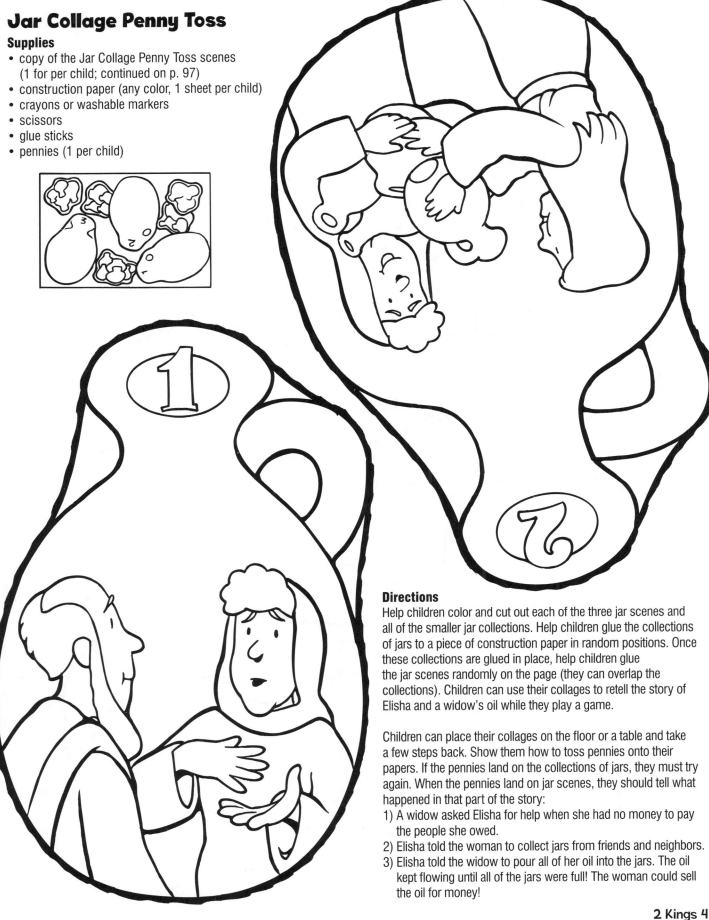

Directions

Help children color and cut out each of the three jar scenes and all of the smaller jar collections. Help children glue the collections of jars to a piece of construction paper in random positions. Once these collections are glued in place, help children glue the jar scenes randomly on the page (they can overlap the collections). Children can use their collages to retell the story of Elisha and a widow's oil while they play a game.

Children can place their collages on the floor or a table and take a few steps back. Show them how to toss pennies onto their papers. If the pennies land on the collections of jars, they must try again. When the pennies land on jar scenes, they should tell what happened in that part of the story:

1) A widow asked Elisha for help when she had no money to pay the people she owed.
2) Elisha told the woman to collect jars from friends and neighbors.
3) Elisha told the widow to pour all of her oil into the jars. The oil kept flowing until all of the jars were full! The woman could sell the oil for money!

2 Kings 4

Elisha and a Widow's Oil

Jar Collage Penny Toss
(continued)

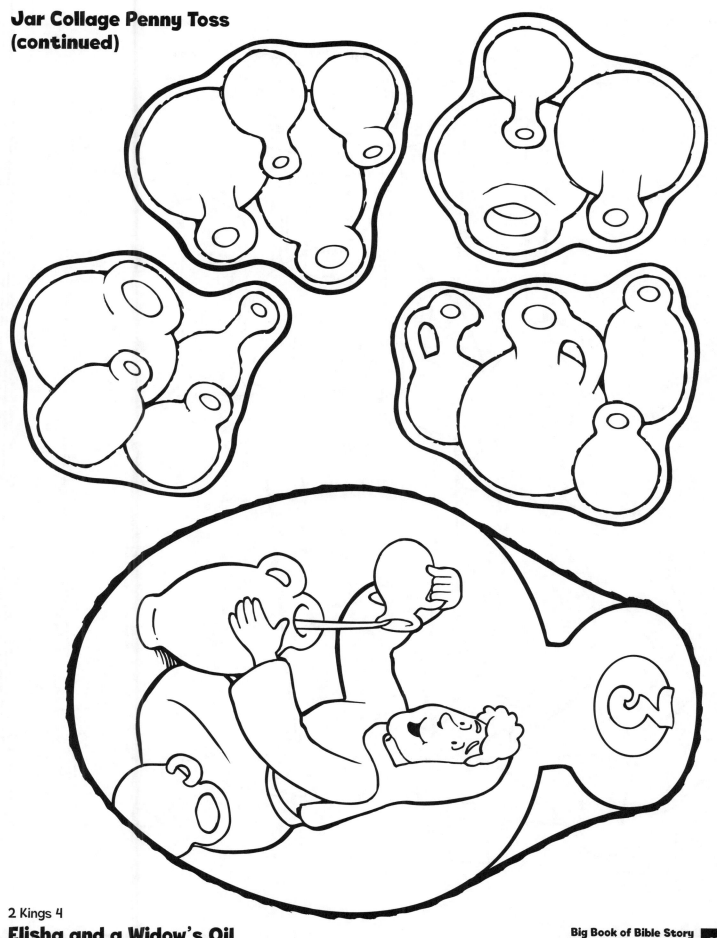

2 Kings 4

Elisha and a Widow's Oil

Big Book of Bible Story
Coloring Activities for Early Childhood
© David C Cook. Permission granted to photocopy for ministry purposes only.

Elisha and a Shunammite Family

Roof Room Stand-Up Scene

Supplies

- copy of the Roof Room Stand-Up Scene furniture pieces (1 per child)
- copy of the Elisha, the Shunammite woman, and the husband stand-up figures on p. 101 (1 per child)
- construction paper (1 sheet per child)
- crayons or washable markers
- scissors
- glue sticks

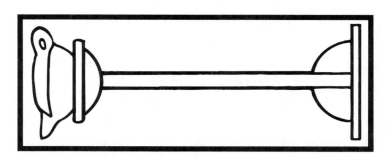

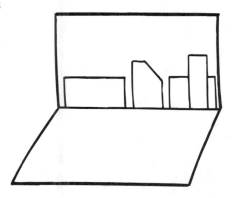

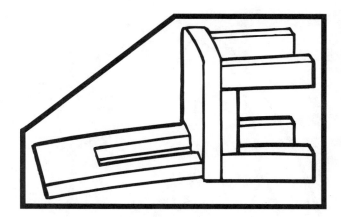

Directions

Help children color and cut out the furniture pieces. Show children how to fold a piece of construction paper in half widthwise and set the paper up so that it resembles a floor and wall (see the example). Glue the furniture pieces to the wall area of the paper. Color and cut out the stand-up puppets of Elisha, the Shunammite woman, and her husband. Fold the bases of the puppets on the dotted lines so they stand up. Place the three figures in the stand-up scene and use them to retell the story of Elisha and the Shunammite family:

1) The Shunammite woman and her husband prepared a room for Elisha (show the woman and her husband).
2) Elisha stayed in the room (show Elisha).
3) Elisha told the Shunammite woman she would have a son (show Elisha and the woman).

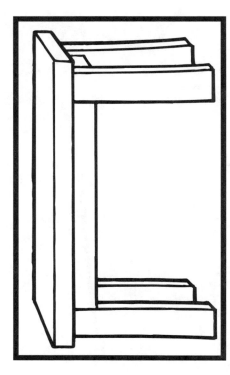

2 Kings 4

Elisha and a Shunammite Family

Elisha and the Shunammite's Son

Shunammite Family Stick Puppets

Supplies

- copy of the Shunammite Family Stick Puppets (1 per child)
- crayons or washable markers
- scissors
- jumbo craft sticks (4 per child)
- tape

Directions

Help children color and cut out the stick puppets (cut along the dotted lines at the bases of Elisha, the mother, and the husband so that they can be used as stick puppets rather than stand-up puppets). Help children attach their puppets to separate craft sticks. Children can use the puppets to retell the story of Elisha and the Shunammite's son:

1) The boy was sick and his father sent him to his mother.
2) The boy died and the mother went to visit Elisha to ask for his help.
3) Elisha came and prayed for the boy and God brought the boy back to life.

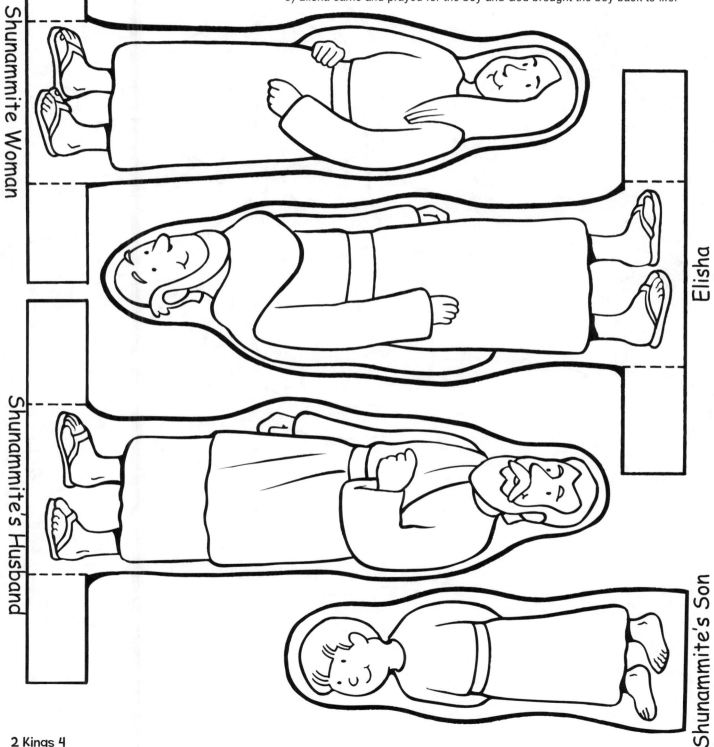

Shunammite Woman

Elisha

Shunammite's Husband

Shunammite's Son

2 Kings 4

Elisha and the Shunammite's Son

Big Book of Bible Story
Coloring Activities for Early Childhood
© David C Cook. Permission granted to photocopy for ministry purposes only.

Elisha and Naaman

Elisha and Naaman Finger Puppets

Supplies

- copy of the Elisha and Naaman Finger Puppets (1 per child)
- crayons or washable markers
- scissors
- tape

Directions

Help children color and cut out the five finger puppets. Tape the puppets to fit around the children's fingers (one per finger). Place sick Naaman on the thumb, Naaman's master on the first finger, the king on the middle finger, Elisha on the ring finger, and healed Naaman on the little finger. Children can use the finger puppets to retell the story of Elisha and Naaman:

1) Naaman was sick (hold up thumb).
2) Naaman wanted to get well and went to see his master (add the first finger).
3) Naaman's master wanted him to get well and sent him to the king (add the middle finger).
4) The king could not help Naaman and sent him to Elisha (add the ring finger).
5) Elisha told Naaman to dip in the Jordan River seven times and he would be healed (bend the thumb up and down seven times and then add the little finger showing the healed Naaman).

Naaman's Master

The King

Elisha

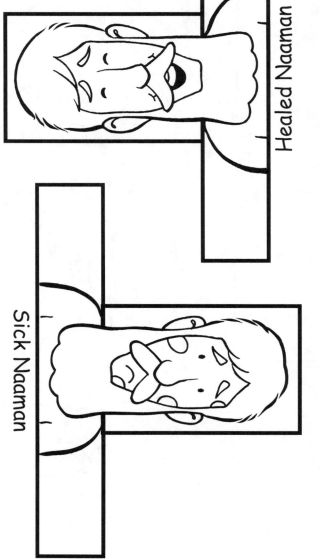

Healed Naaman

Sick Naaman

2 Kings 5

Elisha and Naaman

Big Book of Bible Story
Coloring Activities for Early Childhood
© David C Cook. Permission granted to photocopy for ministry purposes only.

Josiah Reads God's Word

Josiah Story Wheel

Supplies
- copy of the Josiah Story Wheel and cover
  (1 per child; continued on p. 106)
- crayons or washable markers
- scissors
- hole punch
- paper fasteners (1 per child)

Directions
Help children color and cut out the story wheel and cover. Punch a hole through the center of both the cover and the wheel where it is indicated by the open circle. Attach the cover over the wheel using a paper fastener. Children can turn the wheels and look through the openings as they retell the story of Josiah reading God's Word to the people:

1) Josiah was eight years old when he became king.
2) A book of God's law was found in the temple.
3) Josiah read God's Word to the people and he obeyed God all his life.

2 Kings 22–23
Josiah Reads God's Word

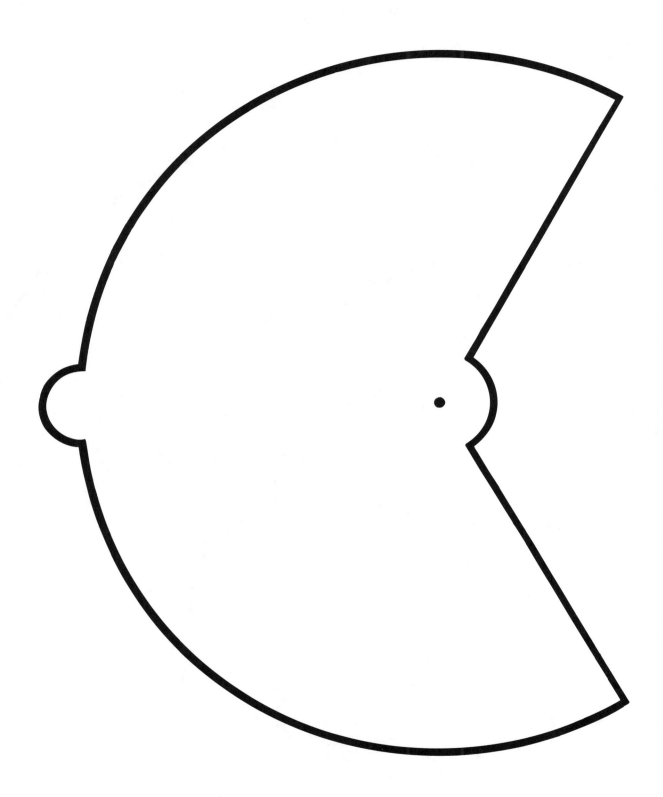

Big Book of Bible Story
Coloring Activities for Early Childhood
© David C Cook. Permission granted to photocopy for ministry purposes only.

12 Kings 22–23
Josiah Reads God's Word

Jehoshaphat Asks for God's Help

Praying Hands Book

Supplies

- copy of the Praying Hands Book (1 per child)
- crayons or washable markers
- scissors

Directions

Help children color and cut out the Praying Hands Book around the solid edge. Fold the book in half on the dotted line so that the praying hands and scene 3 are behind scenes 1 and 2. Fold the book in half again on the dotted line so that scenes 1 and 2 are folded inside with the praying hands showing as the cover of the book (see the example). Children can use the books to tell about Jehoshaphat asking God for help:

1) King Jehoshaphat listened to and obeyed God.
2) The king prayed to God when he needed help.
3) Jehoshaphat worshiped God because God helped him.

2 Chronicles 17, 20

Jehoshaphat Asks for God's Help

Nehemiah Rebuilds the Wall

Wall Mobile

Supplies

- copy of the Wall Mobile pieces (1 per child; continued on p. 111)
- crayons or washable markers
- scissors
- hole punch
- yarn or twine
- card stock (optional)

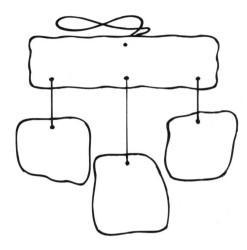

Directions

Help children color and cut out each mobile piece. Using a hole punch, punch out all of the open circles (seven total). Tie each mobile rock scene to the top mobile wall piece through the holes using yarn or twine (see the example). Tie another piece of yarn or twine to the top circle in the wall piece so the mobiles can be hung. Children can use the wall mobiles to tell about Nehemiah rebuilding the wall:

1) Nehemiah was sad that the wall around Jerusalem was broken down. He wanted to rebuild the wall.
2) Nehemiah and the people agreed to rebuild the wall and went right to work.
3) The wall was completed and Nehemiah and the people were happy.

Optional: Copy the mobile pieces on card stock to make them sturdier.

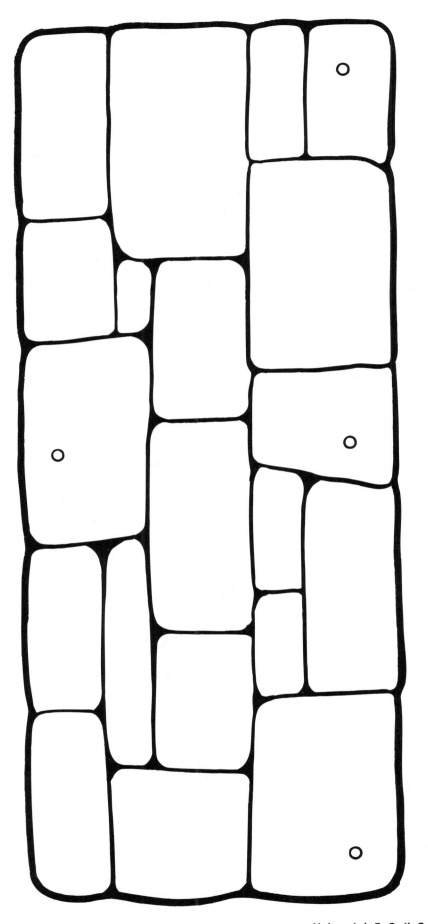

Nehemiah 1–2, 4, 6

Nehemiah Rebuilds the Wall

Wall Mobile (continued)

Big Book of Bible Story
Coloring Activities for Early Childhood
© David C Cook. Permission granted to photocopy for ministry purposes only.

Esther Helps God's People

Esther Crown and Mordecai Hat

Supplies

- copy of the Esther Crown and Mordecai Hat (1 per child)
- crayons or markers
- scissors
- construction paper strips (2" wide and 12" long; 1 per child; any color)
- tape
- glue sticks
- various decorative embellishments (glitter, sequins, beads, gems, stickers (optional)

Directions

Help children color and cut out the crown and hat. Tape a construction paper strip to one side of each hat and crown. Size each hat and crown to fit the size of each child's head. Tape the other end of the construction paper strip to each hat and crown to make headpieces that can be worn. Children can use the crowns and hats to retell the story of Queen Esther helping others as they pretend to be King Xerxes, Mordecai, or Queen Esther.

Esther 2—5, 7—8

Esther Helps God's People

Daniel and His Friends Obey God

Daniel Placemats

Supplies

- copy of the Daniel Placemat pieces (1 per child)
- construction paper (any color, 1 sheet per child)
- black permanent marker
- crayons or washable markers
- scissors
- glue sticks
- clear adhesive covering *(optional)*

Directions

Before class write "We Can Obey God" at the top of each sheet of construction paper (the paper should be laying horizontally when you write these words, like a placemat).

During class help children color and cut out the three scenes. Help children attach the scenes to a piece of construction paper with the words "We Can Obey God" written across the top. Children can use the placemats to retell the story of Daniel and his friends obeying God:

1) Daniel and his friends were told by the king to eat something that God did not want them to eat.
2) Daniel and his friends chose to eat only vegetables rather than disobey God.
3) Daniel and his friends were very healthy and served the king.

Optional: You may want use clear adhesive covering over the placemats so that they last longer.

Daniel 1

Daniel and His Friends Obey God

Daniel's Friends Worship Only God

Fiery Furnace Pop-Up Card

Supplies

- copy of the Fiery Furnace Pop-Up Card (1 per child)
- crayons or washable markers
- scissors

Directions

Help children color the Pop-Up Cards. Cut out the cards along the solid outside lines (do not cut along any dotted lines). Help children fold each card along the horizontal dotted line so the scenes are back to back (see the example). Fold the pop-up piece along the dotted lines while folding the card in half so when the card is closed the pop-up piece is folded inside. When the card is opened, the piece will pop up. Children can use the cards to retell the story of Shadrach, Meshach, and Abednego worshipping only God:

1) The king ordered everyone to bow down to a statue.

2) Shadrach, Meshach, and Abednego would not bow down to the statue so they were thrown into a fiery furnace. God kept them safe and was with them in the furnace.

3) Shadrach, Meshach, and Abednego were not hurt because they obeyed God.

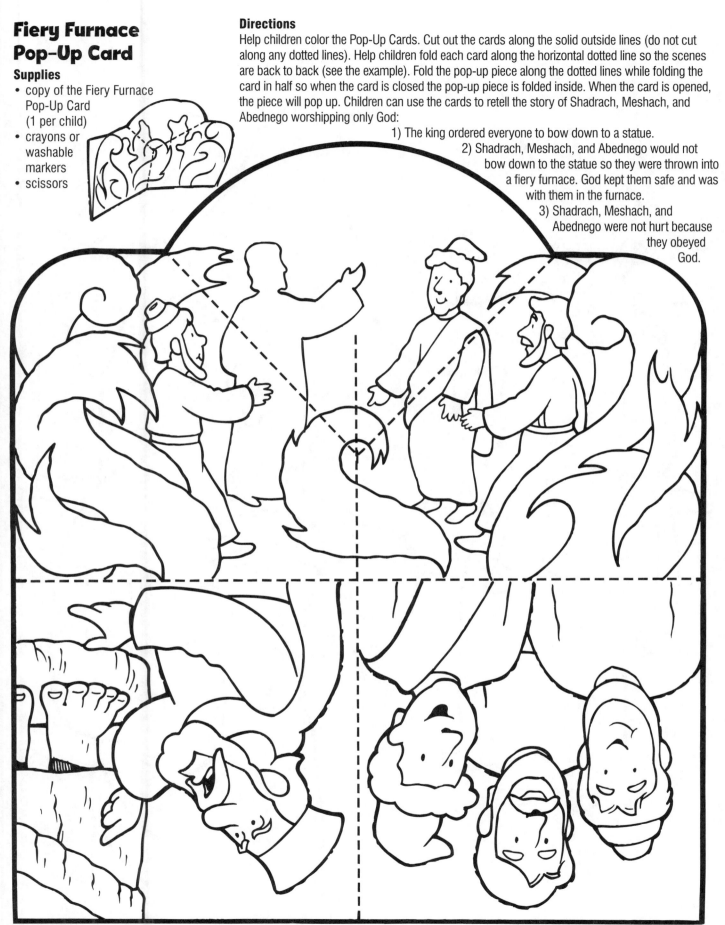

Daniel 3

Daniel's Friends Worship Only God

Daniel and the Handwriting on the Wall

Chain Necklace

Supplies

- copy of the Chain Necklace strips (1 per child)
- crayons or washable markers
- scissors
- tape
- construction paper (purple and yellow, several sheets of each)

Directions

Before class cut several strips of yellow and purple construction paper for each child to use in his or her chain necklace. These strips will lengthen the necklaces so that they can be worn by the children as they retell the story.

Help children color and cut out each story strip along the solid lines. Loop the strips together to form a chain as shown in the example. Place the strips in order according to the events shown on each strip:
1) The king held a banquet and everyone ate and drank at the feast.
2) A hand appeared and wrote a message on the wall.
3) Daniel was called to tell the king what the message said.
4) Daniel told the king that God has power over everything and to worship God only.

Help children add yellow and purple links to their chains using the precut strips. Tell the children that these strips are reminders that Daniel was given a gold chain and a purple robe as a reward for helping the king understand the handwriting. When the chains are long enough, help children attach the two ends together to make story necklaces that the children can wear.

Worship Only God

Daniel 5

Daniel and the Handwriting on the Wall

 Big Book of Bible Story
Coloring Activities for Early Childhood
© David C Cook. Permission granted to photocopy for ministry purposes only.

Daniel and the Lions' Den

Daniel and Lion Puppets

Supplies

- copy of the Daniel and Lion Puppets (1 per child)
- paper lunch bags (2 per child)
- crayons or washable markers
- scissors
- glue
- yarn *(optional: brown and yellow)*
- large wiggle eyes *(optional)*

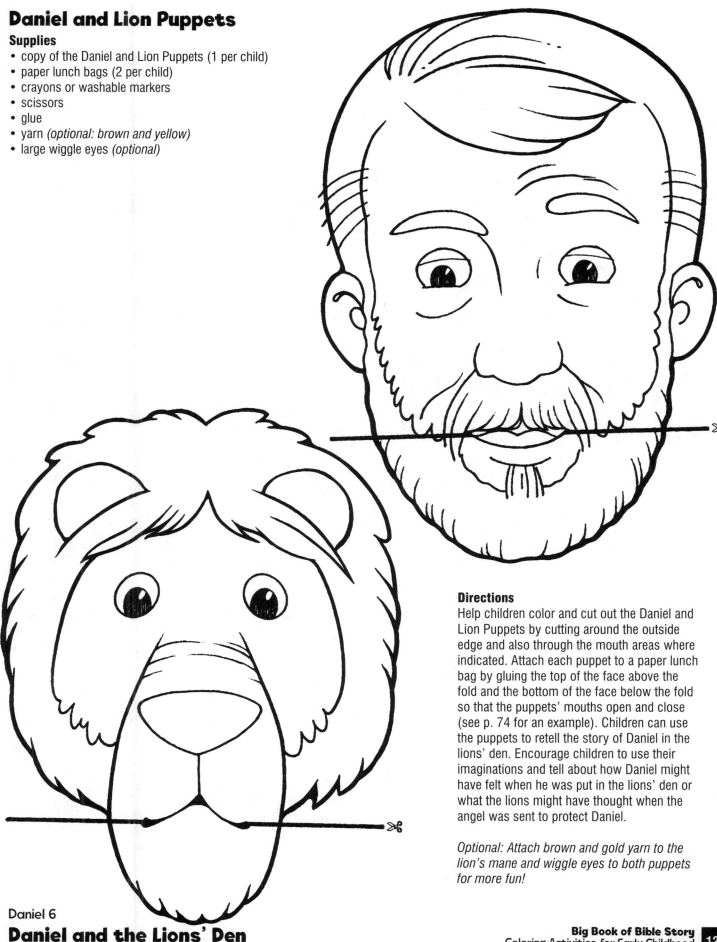

Directions

Help children color and cut out the Daniel and Lion Puppets by cutting around the outside edge and also through the mouth areas where indicated. Attach each puppet to a paper lunch bag by gluing the top of the face above the fold and the bottom of the face below the fold so that the puppets' mouths open and close (see p. 74 for an example). Children can use the puppets to retell the story of Daniel in the lions' den. Encourage children to use their imaginations and tell about how Daniel might have felt when he was put in the lions' den or what the lions might have thought when the angel was sent to protect Daniel.

Optional: Attach brown and gold yarn to the lion's mane and wiggle eyes to both puppets for more fun!

Daniel 6

Daniel and the Lions' Den

Jonah Tells about God

Bag Whale

Supplies

- copy of the Bag Whale and story pieces (1 per child; continued on p. 124)
- crayons or washable markers
- scissors
- paper lunch bags (1 per child)
- glue sticks

Directions

Help children color and cut out both of the whales, the boat, and the Jonah figure. Attach one whale to one side of a paper lunch bag so the whale's mouth is facing the opening of the bag. Repeat this with the other whale on the other side of the bag in the same direction (see the example). Cut off the top part of the paper bag so it is even with the whale's mouth. Children can use their Bag Whales to retell the story of Jonah:

1) Jonah got on a ship to run away from God (show the boat)
2) It started to storm and the people threw Jonah off of the boat (show Jonah jumping off of the boat).
3) A large fish swallowed Jonah (put Jonah into the bag)
4) Jonah prayed inside the fish and the fish spit Jonah out (pull Jonah out of the bag).
5) Jonah obeyed God and went where God told him to go (show Jonah walking away).

Children can use the Bag Whales to hold their story pieces until the next time they retell the story.

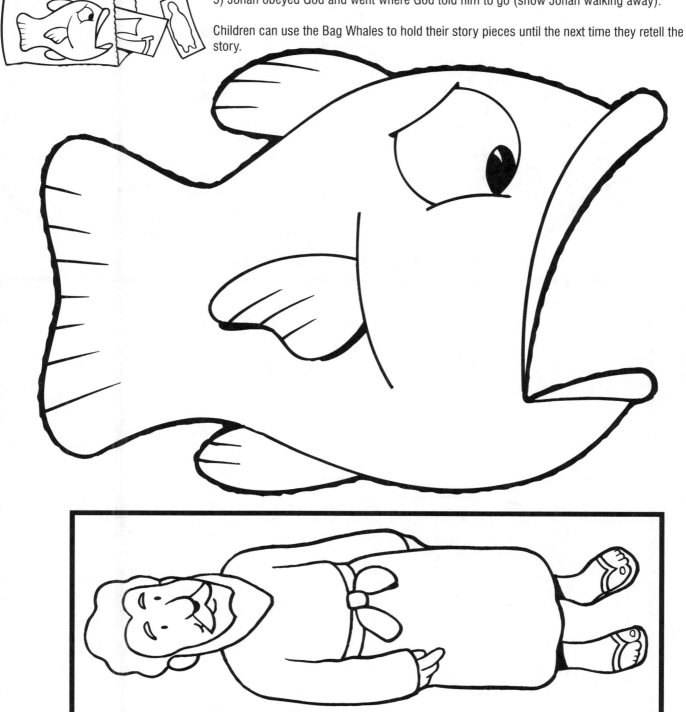

Jonah 1–3

Jonah Tells about God

Bag Whale (continued)

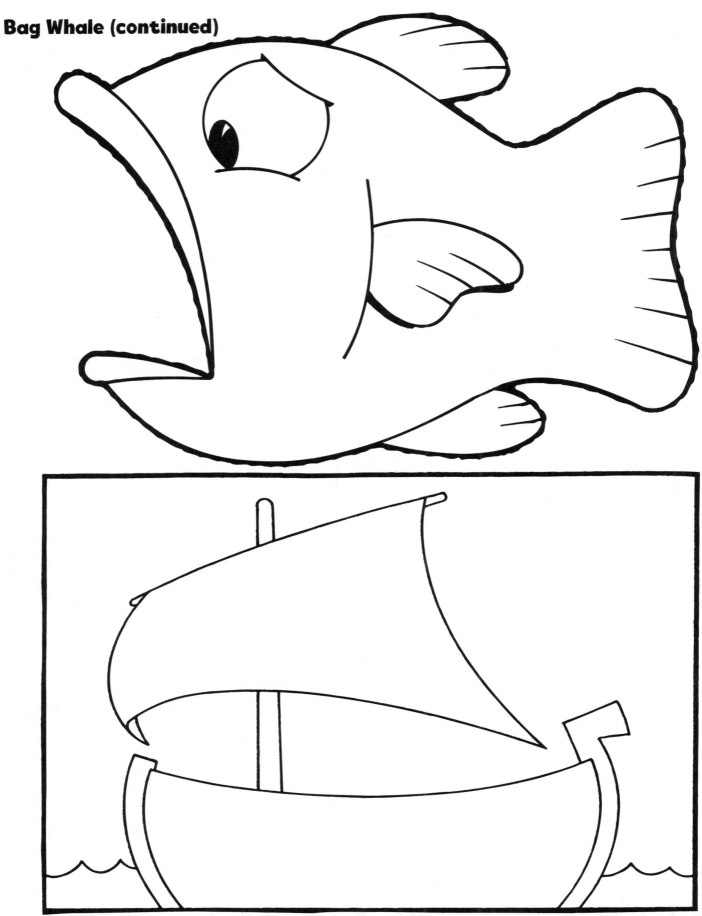

Jonah 1–3:
Jonah Tells about God

An Angel Announces Jesus' Birth

Good News Envelope

Directions

Help children color and cut out the envelope pattern around the outside edge (do not cut on the dotted lines). Fold the envelope flaps in along the dotted lines in the order in which they are numbered. Assist children in writing the name of someone with whom they would like to share the good news of Jesus' birth on the front of their folded envelopes. Children can use the envelopes to retell the story of an angel announcing Jesus' birth to Mary and Joseph.

Supplies
- copy of the Good News Envelope (1 per child)
- crayons or washable markers
- scissors

Matthew 1; Luke 1

An Angel Announces Jesus' Birth

An Angel Brings Special News

Big Book of Bible Story
Coloring Activities for Early Childhood 127
© David C Cook. Permission granted to photocopy for ministry purposes only.

Special News Story Bag

Supplies

- copy of the Special News Story Bag (1 per child)
- crayons or washable markers
- scissors
- paper lunch bags (1 per child)
- glue sticks

Directions

Help children color and cut out the story bag cover and the three scenes. Assist children as they use glue or glue sticks to attach the cover to the front of a paper lunch bag as shown in the example. Children can place their story scenes inside the Special News Story Bags. As they pull the scenes from their bags, they can retell the story of an angel bringing special news:

1) An angel delivered the special news to Joseph in a dream.
2) The angel came to Mary and told her the special news that Jesus would be born.
3) Mary was happy and sang a song after she heard the special news.

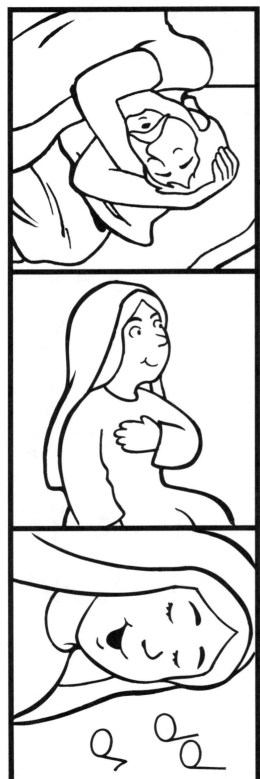

Story Bag Cover   Matthew 1; Luke 1

An Angel Brings Special News

Jesus Is Born

Jesus' Birth Picture Pocket

Supplies

- copy of the Jesus' Birth Picture Pocket and story figures (1 per child; continuted on p. 131)
- crayons or washable markers
- scissors
- construction paper
- glue or glue sticks
- tape

Directions

Help children color and cut out the picture pocket and story figures. Lay a piece of construction paper in front of each child (vertically) and help children glue the background scene to the paper (toward the top). Show children how to fold the bottom portion of the construction paper back and tape it behind the scene to form a pocket (see the example). Children can place the story pieces in the pocket and pull them out as they retell the story of Jesus' birth.

Big Book of Bible Story
Coloring Activities for Early Childhood
© David C Cook. Permission granted to photocopy for ministry purposes only.

Luke 1–2
Jesus Is Born

Luke 1–2

Jesus Is Born

Big Book of Bible Story
Coloring Activities for Early Childhood
© David C Cook. Permission granted to photocopy for ministry purposes only.

A Special Baby Is Born

Lift-and-Look Stable Scenes

Supplies

- copy of the Lift-and-Look Stable Scenes (1 per child)
- construction paper (1 sheet of brown for every 3 children)
- crayons or washable markers
- scissors
- tape)

Directions

Before class, cut four rectangles out of brown construction paper for each child. Each rectangle should be 2½" by 3".

During class, help children color and cut out the stable. Help children put tape on one long edge of each of the construction paper rectangles and tape that edge to one side of each of the square scenes.

Show children how to fold open each flap to reveal the picture underneath (see the example). Children can open the flaps as they retell the story of who was in the stable the night Jesus was born.

Luke 2

A Special Baby Is Born

Big Book of Bible Story
Coloring Activities for Early Childhood   **133**
© David C Cook. Permission granted to photocopy for ministry purposes only.

Big Book of Bible Story
Coloring Activities for Early Childhood
© David C Cook. Permission granted to photocopy for ministry purposes only.

Shepherds Hear Special News

Shepherd's Special News Book

Supplies

- copy of the Shepherds' Special News Book (1 per child)
- crayons or washable markers
- scissors

Directions

Help children color the pictures in the book. Help children cut out the book along the outside border (do not cut on the dotted lines). Fold the book in half lengthwise along the long dotted line so that the scenes are back to back. Fold the book in half again along the short dotted line so that the long scene is folded inside. The picture of the angels should be on the front and the picture of the two men should be on the back. Children can use their books to retell the story of the shepherds hearing the special news of Jesus' birth:

1) Angels appeared to the shepherds while they were in the fields.
2) The shepherds traveled to find baby Jesus.
3) The shepherds told others what they had seen.

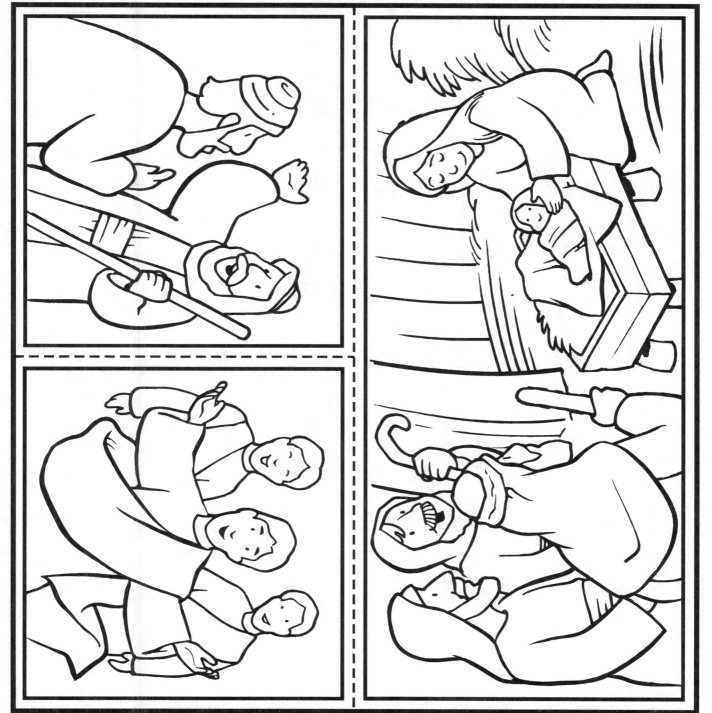

Luke 2

Shepherds Hear Special News

Shepherds Visit Jesus

Shepherds Visit Pamphlet

Step 1

Step 2

Step 3

Supplies

- copy of the Shepherds Visit Pamphlet (1 per child)
- crayons or washable markers
- scissors

Directions

Help children color and cut out the Shepherds Visit Pamphlet. Show children how to fold the pamphlet along the dotted lines. Fold the pamphlet in half lengthwise along the long dotted line so the scenes are back-to-back (three scenes on each side). Lay the pamphlet down so that scene 3 is in front of you. Fold scene 2 in. Fold scene 1 in so that it becomes the cover of the pamphlet (see the examples). Children can use the pamphlets to tell others about the angels bringing good news of Jesus' birth to the shepherds and the shepherds visiting baby Jesus.

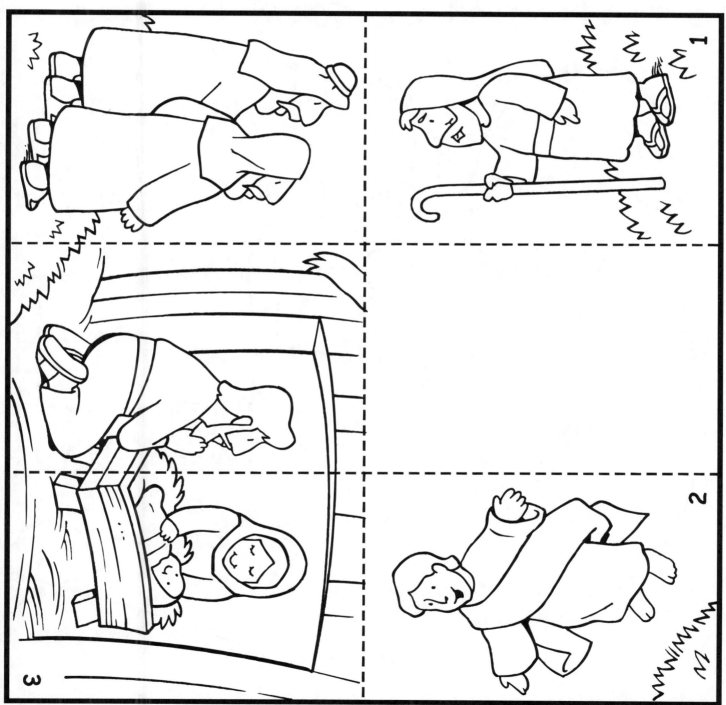

Luke 2

Shepherds Visit Jesus

Big Book of Bible Story
Coloring Activities for Early Childhood
© David C Cook. Permission granted to photocopy for ministry purposes only.

Simeon and Anna See Jesus

Simeon and Anna Puzzle

Supplies
- copy of the Simeon and Anna Puzzle (1 per child; preferably on white card stock)
- crayons or washable markers
- scissors

Directions
Help children color and cut out the puzzle pieces. Children can assemble the puzzle to tell about Mary and Joseph bringing Jesus to the temple. They can also tell about Simeon and Anna seeing Jesus and praising God.

Luke 2

Simeon and Anna See Jesus

Wise Men Worship a Special Baby

Wise Men Stand-Up Scene

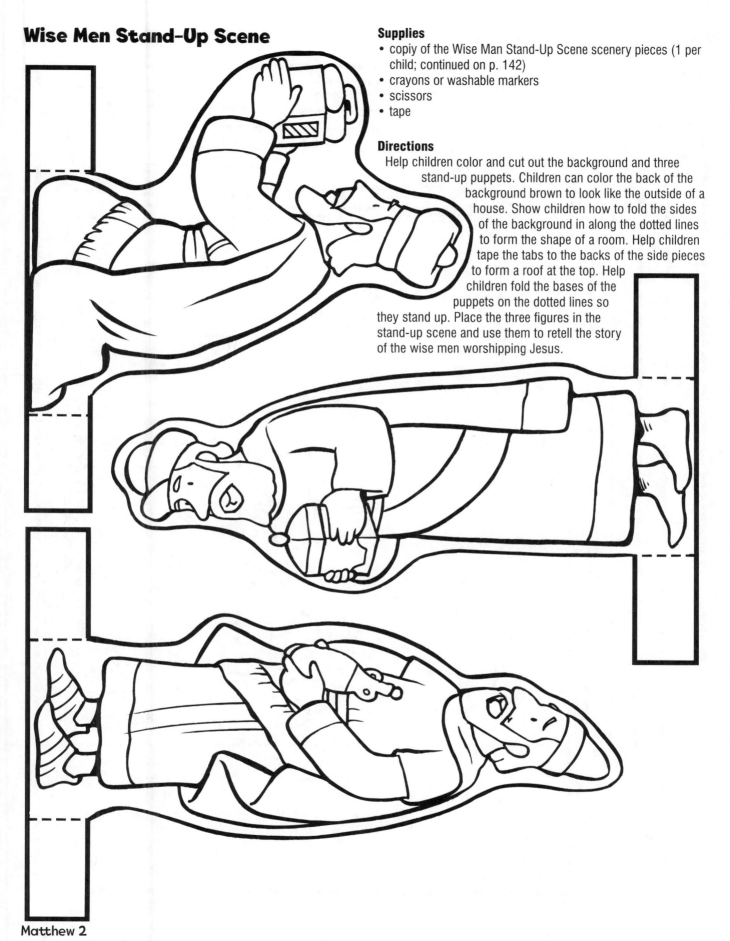

Supplies

- copiy of the Wise Man Stand-Up Scene scenery pieces (1 per child; continued on p. 142)
- crayons or washable markers
- scissors
- tape

Directions

Help children color and cut out the background and three stand-up puppets. Children can color the back of the background brown to look like the outside of a house. Show children how to fold the sides of the background in along the dotted lines to form the shape of a room. Help children tape the tabs to the backs of the side pieces to form a roof at the top. Help children fold the bases of the puppets on the dotted lines so they stand up. Place the three figures in the stand-up scene and use them to retell the story of the wise men worshipping Jesus.

Matthew 2

Wise Men Worship a Special Baby

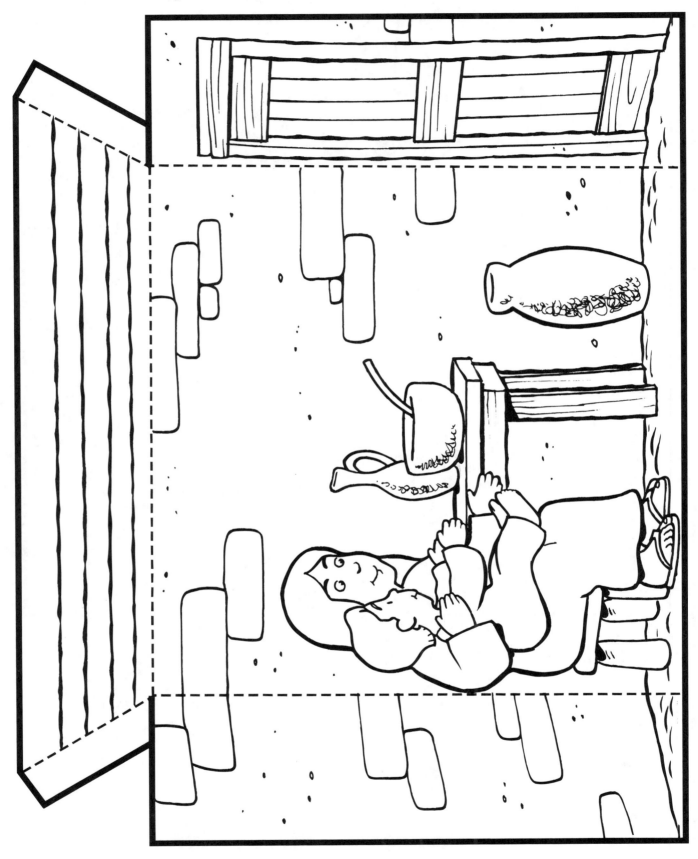

Matthew 2

Wise Men Worship a Special Baby

Wise Men Worship Jesus

Star Pennant

Supplies

- copy of the Star Pennant scenes (1 per child)
- construction paper (black or dark blue)
- crayons or washable markers
- scissors
- hole punch
- glue sticks
- star stickers
- yarn

Directions

Before class cut a sheet of construction paper (black or dark blue) into three sections across the width of the sheet so each piece is 9" tall and 4" wide. Cut one sheet per child so each child will have three separate pieces measuring 9" x 4" each.

Help children color and cut out the Star Pennant scenes. Show children how to fold each of the three pieces of construction paper in half and punch two holes at the top of each fold (see step 1 of the example). Help children glue the pennant scenes inside each of the three construction paper folds (see step 2 of the example). Allow children to add star stickers to the front flap of each scene as a reminder that God used a star to guide the wise men to baby Jesus. Children can string yarn through the holes in the top of each scene so the scenes appear in order and can be hung (see step 3 of the example). Children can use their Star Pennants to tell about the wise men talking to King Herod about baby Jesus, traveling to find the baby, and worshipping Jesus when they found Him.

Step 1   Step 2

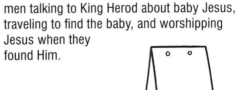

Step 3

Big Book of Bible Story
Coloring Activities for Early Childhood

Matthew 2

Wise Men Worship Jesus

Jesus as a Boy

Jesus as a Boy Book

Supplies

- copy of the Jesus as a Boy Book (1 per child)
- crayons or washable markers
- scissors

Directions

Help the children color and cut out the Jesus as a Boy Book. Show children how to fold the book in half so scenes 1 and 4 are behind scenes 2 and 3. Lay the book down so scenes 2 and 3 are facing you. Fold the book in half so scene 4 is the back of the book and scene 1 is the front (see the example). Children can use the books to retell the story of Jesus as a boy:

1) Jesus went to Jerusalem with His parents when He was 12 years old.
2) Mary and Joseph left to go home without Jesus.
3) Mary and Joseph returned to Jerusalem to look for Jesus.
4) Mary and Joseph found Jesus at the temple talking with the teachers there.

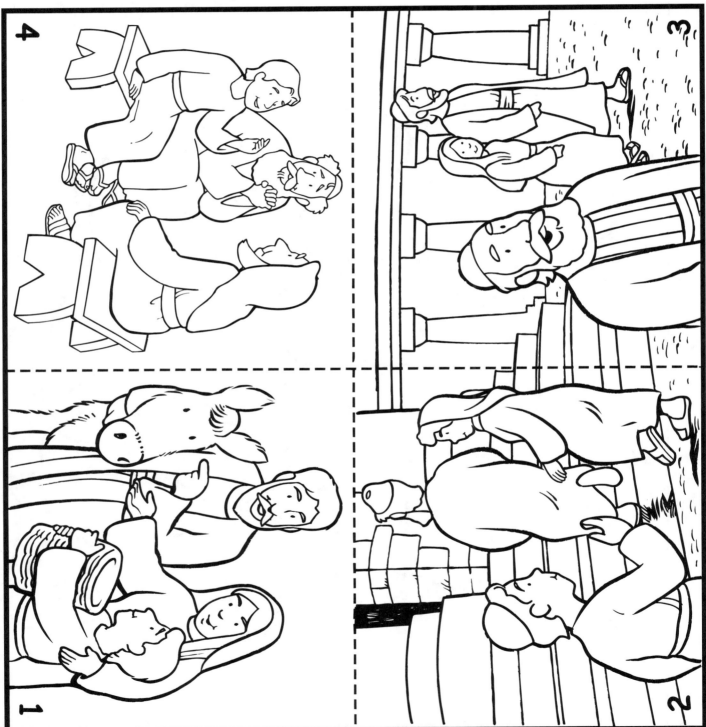

Luke 2

Big Book of Bible Story
Coloring Activities for Early Childhood
© David C Cook. Permission granted to photocopy for ministry purposes only.

Jesus as a Boy

Jesus Is Baptized

Fold-Down Baptism

Supplies

- copy of the Fold-Down Baptism (1 per child)
- crayons or washable markers
- scissors

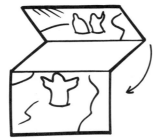

Matthew 3; Mark 1

Jesus Is Baptized

Jesus Is Tempted

Jesus Says No!

Supplies

- copy of the Jesus Says No! scenes and word strips (1 per child)
- crayons or washable markers
- scissors
- construction paper (any color, 1 sheet per child)
- glue sticks
- hole punch
- yarn (any color)

Directions

Before class, cut one piece of construction paper into four equal sections for each child. On one of the pieces, write, "Jesus Says No!"

During class help children color and cut out each scene and word strip. Help children glue each scene to a separate rectangle of construction paper. Under each scene the children should glue the matching word strip. Give each child a small rectangle of construction paper on which the words, "Jesus Says No!" have been written. Help children place all of their construction paper rectangles in order (like a book) according to the numbers in the lower right corners of each scene. Punch holes along the left side of the pages of the book and tie the book together using yarn. Children can use their books to tell about Jesus being in the desert, saying no to each temptation, and reciting verses from God's Word.

Jesus went into the desert to fast and pray.

Satan tried to tempt Jesus to do wrong.

Jesus said verses from God's Word when He was tempted.

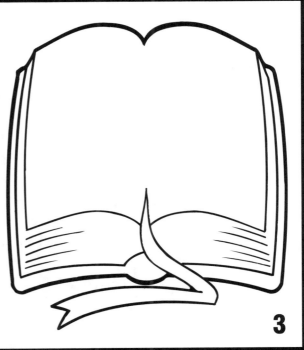

Matthew 4

Jesus Is Tempted

Two Friends Follow Jesus

Following Friends Hand Puppets

Supplies

- copy of the Following Friends Hand Puppets (1 per child)
- crayons or washable markers
- scissors
- tape

Directions

Help children color and cut out the hand puppets. Show the children how to fold the two puppets in half on the dotted lines and tape the sides together so each puppet fits on the child's hand like a mitten. Assist each child in putting the Philip puppet on one hand and the Nathanael puppet on the other hand. Children can use the puppets to retell the story of Philip and Nathanael choosing to follow Jesus. Children can tell about how excited Philip might have been to tell Nathanael about Jesus. Children can also tell about how Nathanael might have felt when Philip told him about Jesus or how he might have felt when Jesus told him that He saw Nathanael under the fig tree.

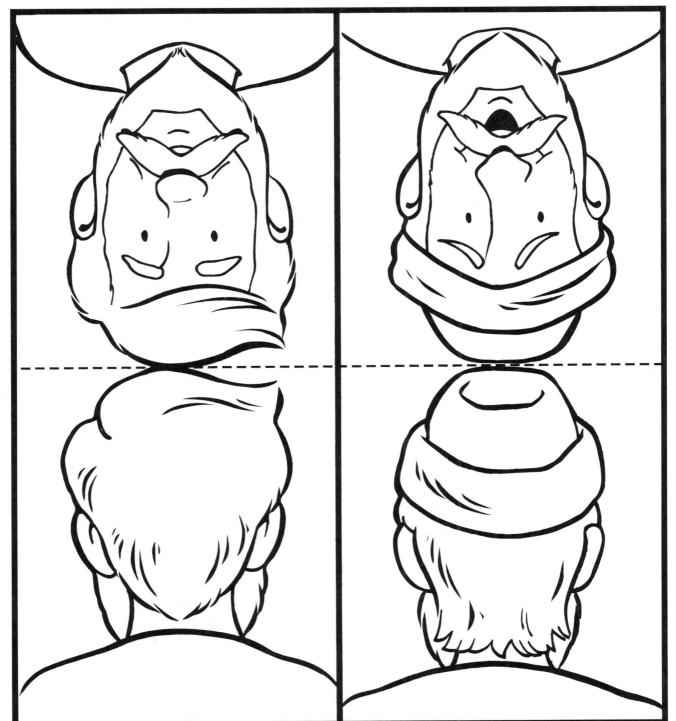

John 1

Two Friends Follow Jesus

Jesus and a Woman from Samaria

Well Mobile

Supplies

- copy of the Well Mobile (preferably on white card stock; 1 per child; continued on p. 155)
- crayons or washable markers
- scissors
- gray or brown construction paper (1 sheet per child)
- glue sticks
- tape
- hole punch
- yarn (any color)

Directions

Help children color and cut out the mobile pieces (the blank rectangle should not be colored). Give each child a piece of construction paper. Show children how to tear the paper into small circles to look like stones. Help children glue their "stones" to the top mobile piece (the long rectangle) to make it look like stones on the side of a well. Have children glue on the side that doesn't have the circles. Once the glue is dry, help children wrap the top mobile pieces into a circle shape and tape it at the seams. Punch holes in each water jar piece and in the top mobile piece where indicated by the open circles. Help children attach the jar scenes to the top of the mobile using varying lengths of yarn. Tie one long piece of yarn through the two holes in the top of the well so that the mobile can be hung. Children can use their Well Mobiles to retell the story of Jesus and a woman from Samaria.

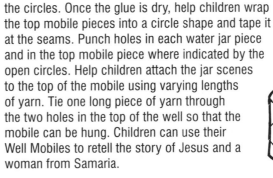

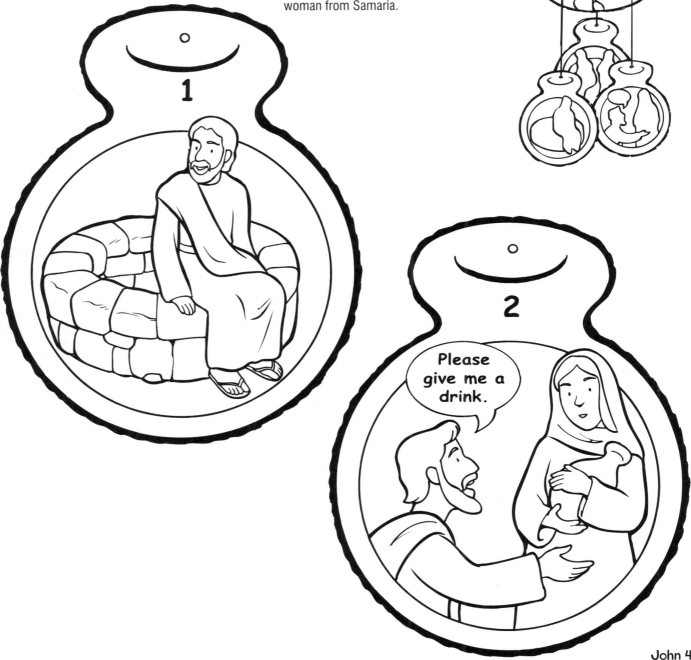

Big Book of Bible Story
Coloring Activities for Early Childhood

John 4

Jesus and a Woman from Samaria

Well Mobile (continued)

3

John 4

Jesus and a Woman from Samaria

Big Book of Bible Story
Coloring Activities for Early Childhood
© David C Cook. Permission granted to photocopy for ministry purposes only.

Jesus Heals an Official's Son

Jesus and Official Finger Leg Puppets

Supplies

- copy of the Jesus and Official Finger Leg Puppets (1 per child; preferably on white card stock)
- crayons or washable markers)
- scissors

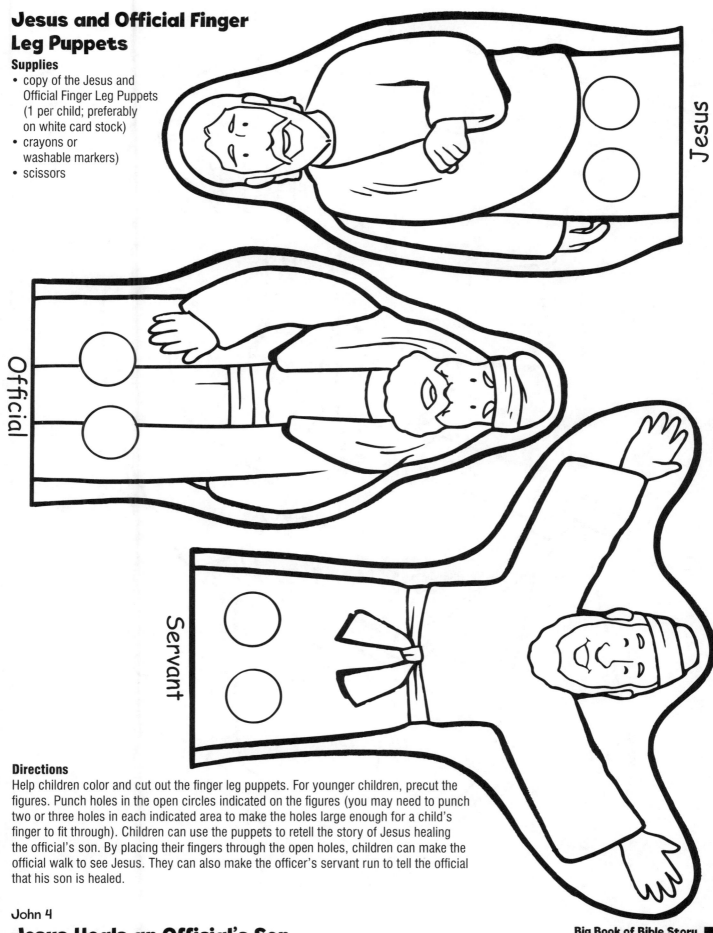

Jesus

Official

Servant

Directions

Help children color and cut out the finger leg puppets. For younger children, precut the figures. Punch holes in the open circles indicated on the figures (you may need to punch two or three holes in each indicated area to make the holes large enough for a child's finger to fit through). Children can use the puppets to retell the story of Jesus healing the official's son. By placing their fingers through the open holes, children can make the official walk to see Jesus. They can also make the officer's servant run to tell the official that his son is healed.

John 4
Jesus Heals an Official's Son

Jesus Begins to Teach

Toss, Travel, and Teach

Supplies

- copy of the Toss, Travel, and Teach pieces (1 per child; continued on p. 160)
- crayons or washable markers
- scissors
- construction paper (any color, 1 sheet per child)
- glue or glue sticks
- pennies or buttons (1 per child)

Directions

Help children color and cut out each of the three scenes showing Jesus and all of the footprint collections. Assist children as they glue the collections of footprints to a piece of construction paper (they can be placed randomly). Then help children glue the scenes showing Jesus randomly on the same page (they can overlap the footprints). See the example. Children can use their collages to play a game. Have children place their collages on the floor or on a table and take a few steps back. They can toss pennies or buttons onto their papers. If their pennies land on a collection of footprints, they can tell about Jesus traveling from town to town as He taught people. If their pennies land on a scene showing Jesus, they can tell about what that scene shows (Jesus taught, Jesus cared about people, Jesus healed sick people).

Matthew 4

Jesus Begins to Teach

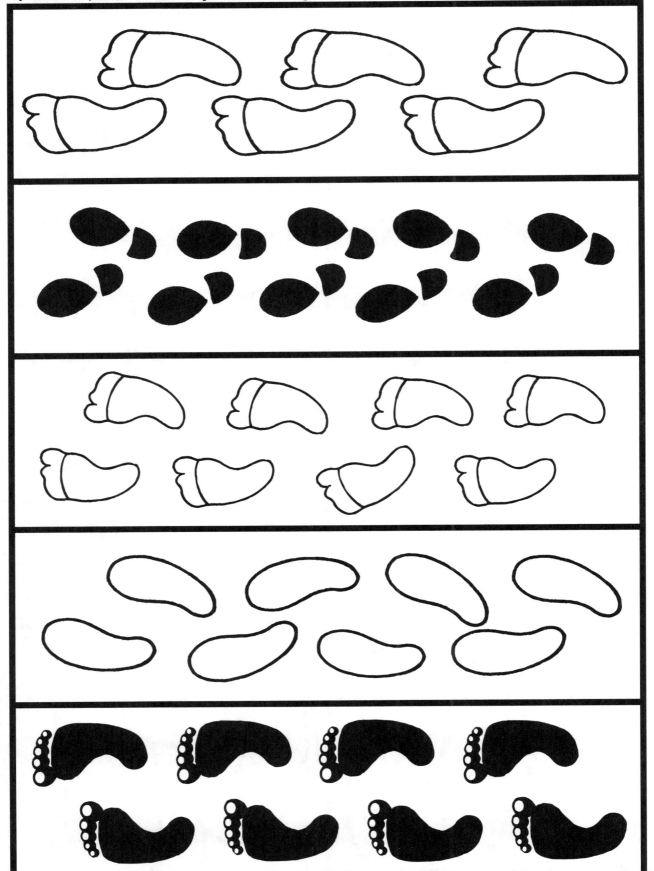

 Big Book of Bible Story
Coloring Activities for Early Childhood
© David C Cook. Permission granted to photocopy for ministry purposes only.

Matthew 4

Jesus Begins to Teach

Fishermen Follow Jesus

Fishermen Finger Puppets

Supplies

- copy of the Fishermen Finger Puppets (1 per child)
- crayons or washable markers
- scissors
- tape

Directions

Help children color and cut out the four finger puppets. Tape the puppets to fit around the children's fingers (one per finger). Place Jesus on the first finger, Simon Peter on the middle finger, James on the ring finger, and John on the little finger (see the example). Children can use the finger puppets to retell the story of Jesus' first followers:

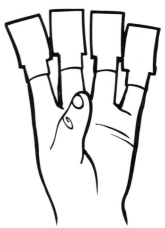

1) Jesus was teaching a large crowd on a shore (show Jesus).
2) Jesus got into Simon Peter's boat to teach because the crowd was so large (show Simon Peter).
3) After Jesus finished speaking, He told Simon Peter where to go to catch fish (show Jesus and Simon Peter).
4) There were so many fish that James and John had to come and help (show James and John).
5) Simon Peter, James, and John were amazed. They left everything and followed Jesus.

Luke 5

Fishermen Follow Jesus

Jesus Heals a Man Who Could Not Walk

Big Book of Bible Story
Coloring Activities for Early Childhood

163

© David C Cook. Permission granted to photocopy for ministry purposes only.

Four Friends Four-Fold Book

Supplies
- copy of the Four Friends Four-Fold Book (1 per child)
- crayons or washable markers
- scissors

Directions

Help children color and cut out the Four Friends Four-Fold book. Children can cut along all of the solid lines (this will include cutting between scenes 1 and 4). Help children fold the book in half so scenes 1 and 4 are behind scenes 2 and 3. Fold the book in half again so scene 1 is on the front and scenes 2 and 3 are folded inside. Children can use the books to retell the story of Jesus healing a man who could not walk (as children come to scene 4 they should fold the scene down so it appears under scene 3 to look like one long scene—see the example):

1) Jesus was speaking to a large crowd.
2) Four friends brought to Jesus a man who could not walk.
3) The friends cut a hole in the roof to lower their friend down because there were so many people crowded inside the house.
4) Jesus healed the man and he could walk.

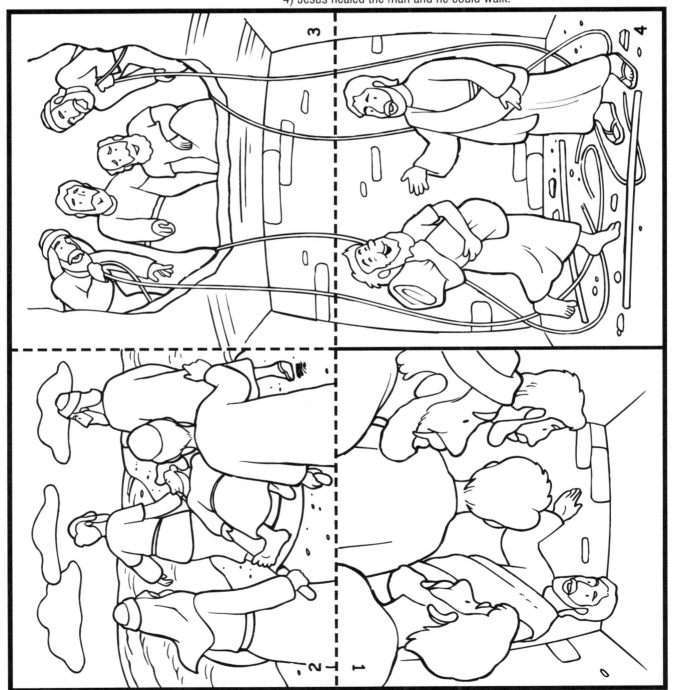

Mark 2; Luke 5

Jesus Heals a Man Who Could Not Walk

Jesus and Matthew

Meal Time Story Wheel

Supplies

- copy of the Meal Time Story Wheel (1 per child)
- copy of the Story Wheel Cover on p. 106 (1 per child)
- crayons or washable markers
- scissors
- hole punch
- paper fasteners (1 per child)
- various food stickers

Directions

Help children color and cut out the Meal Time Story Wheel and the Story Wheel Cover. Place the wheel cover over the story wheel and punch a hole in the center where indicated by the open circle. Place paper fasteners in the center of the story wheels. Children can decorate the covers of their wheels with food stickers as a reminder that Jesus had dinner at Matthew's house. Children can use their story wheels to retell the story of Jesus and Matthew:

1) Jesus called Matthew to follow Him.
2) Jesus ate dinner at Matthew's house.
3) Jesus told the religious leaders why it was important for Him to spend time with Matthew even though others didn't like Matthew and his friends.

Matthew 9; Luke 5

Jesus and Matthew

Jesus Teaches about Pleasing God

Pleasing God Pop-Up Card

Supplies
- copy of the Pleasing God Pop-Up Card (1 per child)
- crayons or washable markers
- scissors

Directions
Help the children color and cut out the pop-up card (cut only on the solid lines, do not cut on dotted lines). Show the children how to fold the card in half along the horizontal dotted line so the scenes are back-to-back. Fold the pop-up piece along the dotted lines so when the card is opened this piece pops up. Fold the card along the center dotted line so that the pop-up piece is folded inside the card (see the example). Children can use the pop-up cards to retell the story of Jesus teaching others about pleasing God:
1) Jesus was teaching the people.
2) Jesus taught that we should pray for our enemies.
3) Jesus taught that we should give to those who are in need.
4) Jesus taught that we should love one another and treat others like we would like to be treated.

Matthew 5–7

Big Book of Bible Story
Coloring Activities for Early Childhood
© David C Cook. Permission granted to photocopy for ministry purposes only.

Jesus Teaches about Pleasing God

Jesus Teaches about Giving

Giving Container

Supplies

- copy of the Giving Container (1 per child)
- crayons or washable markers
- scissors
- tape

Directions

Help children color and then cut out the Giving Container around the outside edge (do not cut on the dotted lines). Show the children how to fold the container along the dotted lines to form the finished shape (see the example). Tape the tab on scene 1 to the back of scene 3 to finish the activity. Children can use the containers to retell the story of Jesus teaching about giving:

1) A poor widow came to the temple one day.
2) The widow gave two coins to the offering. They were all she had.
3) Jesus was happy that she gave everything she had even though she didn't have much.

Children can also use the container to collect money that they would like to give at church.

Matthew 6; Mark 12

Jesus Teaches about Giving

Jesus Heals the Soldier's Servant

Soldier Story Mask

Supplies
- copy of the Soldier Story Mask (1 per child)
- crayons or washable markers
- scissors
- jumbo craft sticks (1 per child)
- tape

Directions
Help children color and cut out the Soldier Story Mask. You may need to cut out the eyes for the children. Assist children in attaching the story masks to craft sticks by taping a stick to the back, bottom portion of each mask (see the example). Children can use the story masks to retell the story of Jesus healing the soldier's servant as they play the part of the soldier. Children can tell about the soldier having such great faith in Jesus that he believed Jesus didn't even have to come to his house for his servant to be healed.

Matthew 8; Luke 7

Jesus Heals the Soldier's Servant

Jesus Brings a Young Man Back to Life

City Gate Story Bag

Supplies

- copy of the City Gate Story Bag (1 per child)
- crayons or washable markers
- scissors
- paper lunch bags (1 per child)
- glue sticks

Directions

Help children color and cut out the city gate and the three scenes. Assist children as they use glue sticks to attach the city gate to the front of a paper lunch bag as shown in the example. Children can place the story scenes inside their City Gate Story Bags. As they pull each scene from the bag, they can retell the story of Jesus bringing a young man back to life.

Luke 7

Big Book of Bible Story
Coloring Activities for Early Childhood

Jesus Brings a Young Man Back to Life

Jesus Stops a Storm

Big Book of Bible Story
Coloring Activities for Early Childhood

175

Fold-Away Storm

Supplies

- copy of the Fold-Away Storm (1 per child)
- crayons or washable markers
- scissors

Directions

Help children color and cut out the Fold-Away Storm around the solid edge (do not cut along the dotted lines). Show children how to fold the page along the top dotted line so only the portions showing Jesus standing in the boat with the wind above Him are visible. Fold the page forward along the remaining dotted line to reveal the portion showing Jesus standing in the boat with the clouds above Him. See the example. Children can use the Fold-Away Storm activity to retell the story of Jesus calming the storm.

Mark 4

Jesus Stops a Storm

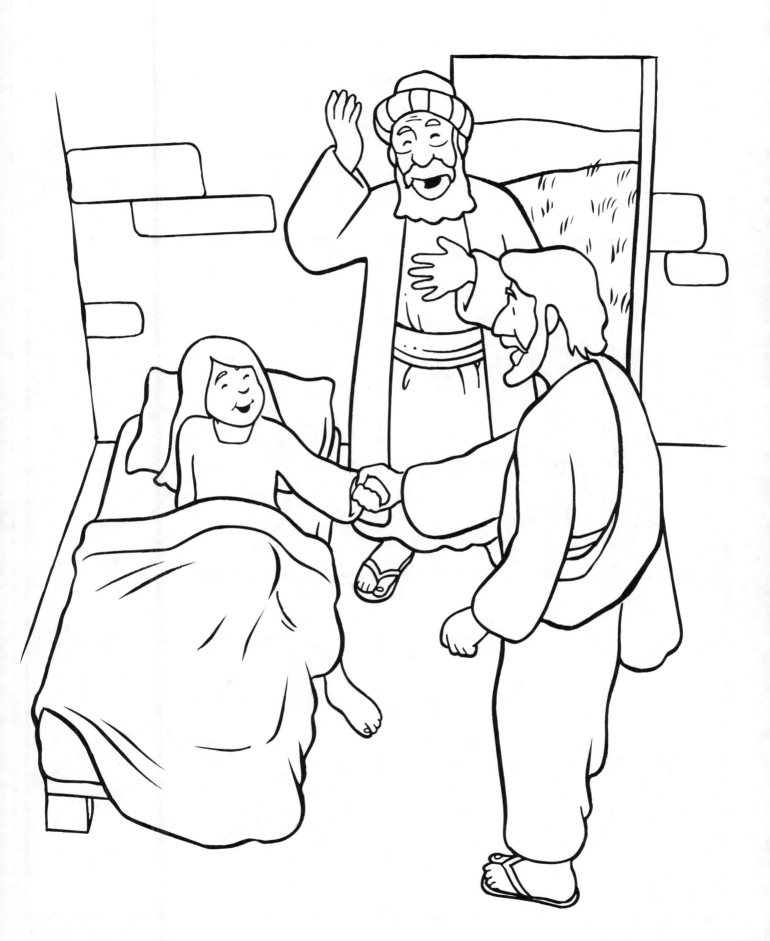

Jesus Heals a Young Girl

Unfolding Healing Scene

Supplies
- copy of the Unfolding Healing Scene square (1 per child)
- crayons or washable markers
- scissors

Directions
Help children color and cut out the square containing the four story scenes (do not cut apart the individual scenes, cut the square as one large piece). Fold the four story scenes on the dotted lines so the scenes are folded inside. As each flap is opened, a scene should appear. Children can use the Unfolding Healing Scene to retell the story of Jesus healing a young girl:

1) A man named Jairus came to ask Jesus to help his sick daughter.
2) Jesus went with Jairus to his house.
3) When Jesus arrived at Jairus's house, the people were crying because the girl had died. Jesus told them not to cry.
4) Jesus went to the girl and told her to stand up. She stood up immediately! The girl's parents were amazed.

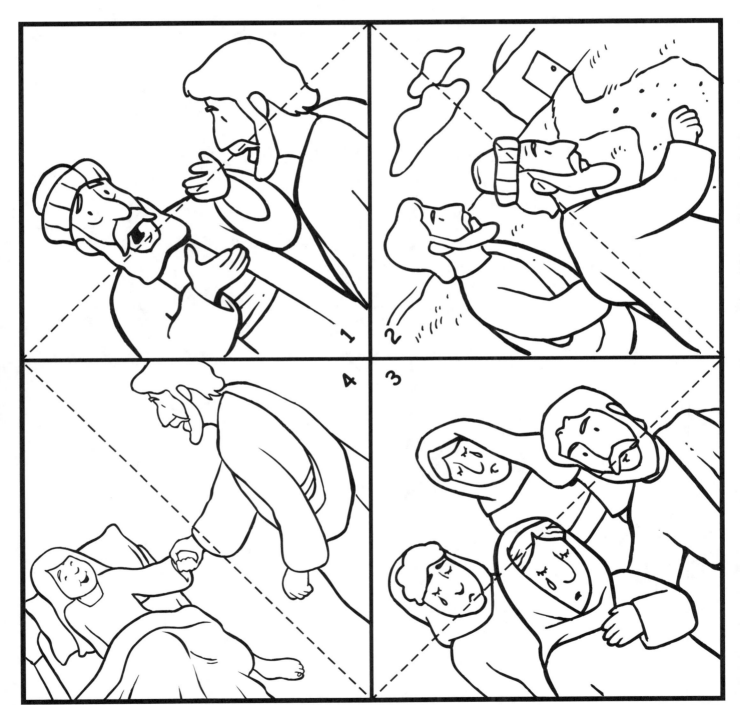

Luke 8

Jesus Heals a Young Girl

Jesus Feeds a Crowd

Feed a Crowd Memory Game

Supplies

- copy of the Feed a Crowd Memory Game pictures and questions (1 per child; preferably on card stock)
- crayons or washable markers
- scissors
- envelopes (1 per child)

Directions

Help children color and cut out the ten story scenes. Children should also cut apart the ten questions and place the questions in their envelopes. Have the children mix up the story scenes and place them facedown on a table or the floor in front of them. Group children in pairs and have them play the game using one set of scenes and questions. One child should draw a question from the envelope. He or she may then turn over two story scenes to try to find the picture that answers the question. If a match is made, he or she may keep the story scene and the matching question in a pile to the side. If not, he or she should turn the two scenes back over, place the question back in the envelope and try again on another turn. Children can take their memory games home and play with family members as they retell the story of Jesus feeding a crowd.

1. Did a few people or many people come to see Jesus?

2. What did the people want to see Jesus do?

3. Was Jesus teaching by a lake or on a hillside?

4. Why did Philip say they couldn't feed the people?

5. Whom did Andrew bring to Jesus?

6. What did the boy have in his lunch?

7. What did Jesus do before He shared the boy's lunch?

8. Who gave the food to all the people?

9. What did the people do when they were given food?

10. How much food was left over?

Big Book of Bible Story
Coloring Activities for Early Childhood

John 6

Jesus Feeds a Crowd

Jesus Walks on Water

Walk along Jesus

Supplies

- copy of the Walk Along Jesus story pieces (preferably on white card stock; 1 per child; continued on p. 183)
- crayons or washable markers
- scissors
- tape
- craft sticks (1 per child)

Directions

Help children color and cut out the three story scenes and the Jesus figure. In scene 3, help children cut a slit where it is indicated by the bold, horizontal line in the end of the boat (a teacher or helper may need to do this for younger children). Help children tape the story scenes together so they appear in order by the numbers in the lower left corners. Help the children tape the Jesus figure to a craft stick. As they retell the story, children should put Jesus in the place of the empty rectangle in each scene. When they come to scene 3, they should insert the Jesus figure through the slit (only showing the top half of His body) so that it looks like He is in the boat with His followers (see the example). Children can use the Walk along Jesus activity to retell the story of Jesus walking on water.

Mark 6; John 6

Jesus Walks on Water

Mark 6
Jesus Walks on Water

Jesus Heals a Man Who Could Not Hear or Speak

Speak and Hear Spinning Scenes

Supplies

- copy of the Speak and Hear Spinning Scenes (1 per child; preferably on white card stock)
- crayons or washable markers
- scissors
- paper fasteners
- paper clips

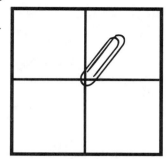

Directions

Help children color and cut out the square game board (do not cut between the scenes). Assist children in attaching paper clips as a spinner to the center of the game using paper fasteners (loose enough for the paper clip to spin freely). Children can spin the paper clip. When the paper clip lands on a scene the children can tell what that scene shows as they retell the story of Jesus healing a man who could not hear or speak:

1) Some people brought a man to Jesus. The man could not hear or speak.
2) Jesus put His fingers in the man's ears.
3) Jesus spit and touched the man's tongue. Jesus looked up to heaven, took a deep breath, and said "Be opened!"
4) The man could hear and speak! The people were amazed!

Mark 7

Jesus Heals a Man Who Could Not Hear or Speak

Big Book of Bible Story
Coloring Activities for Early Childhood
© David C Cook. Permission granted to photocopy for ministry purposes only.

Jesus Heals a Man Born Blind

Man Born Blind Book

Supplies

- copy of the Man Born Blind Book (1 per child)
- crayons or washable markers
- scissors

Directions

Help the children color and cut out the Man Born Blind Book. Show children how to fold the book in half so scenes 1 and 4 are behind scenes 2 and 3. Lay the book so scenes 2 and 3 are facing you. Fold the book in half so scene 4 is the back of the book and scene 1 is the front (see the example). Children can use the books to retell the story of Jesus healing a man born blind:

1) Jesus was walking and saw a man who had been born blind. Jesus spit on the ground and made mud.
2) Jesus put the mud on the man's eyes.
3) Jesus told the man to go and wash in the Pool of Siloam. The man did what Jesus said.
4) The man could see! People asked him what had happened and he told them what Jesus had done for him.

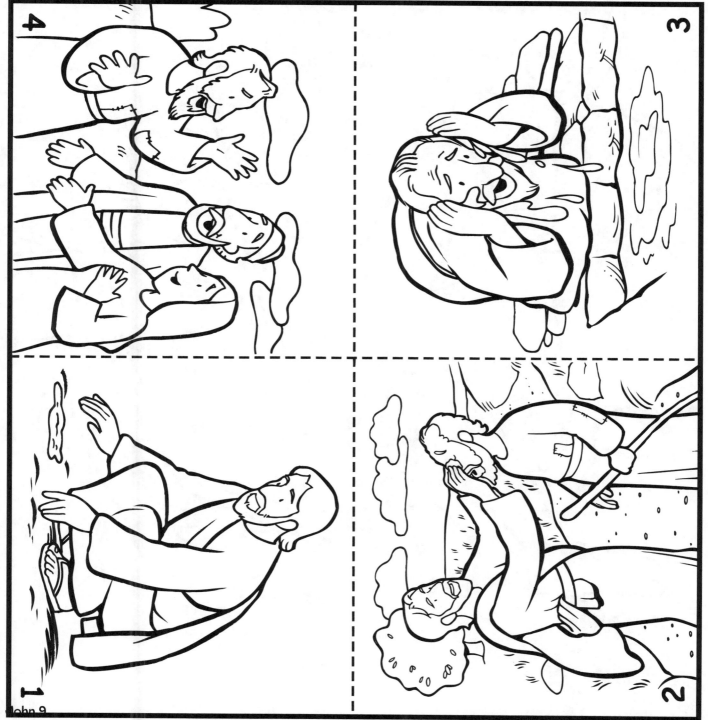

John 9

Jesus Heals a Man Born Blind

Jesus Teaches about Helping

Helping Hands Picture Pocket

Supplies

- copy of the Helping Hands Picture Pocket and story figures (1 per child; continued on p. 190)
- crayons or washable markers
- scissors
- construction paper
- glue or glue sticks
- tape

Directions

Help children color and cut out the picture pocket and story figures. Lay a piece of construction paper in front of each child (vertically) and help children glue the background scene to the paper (toward the top). Show children how to fold the bottom portion of the construction paper back and tape it behind the scene to form a pocket. Children can place the story pieces in the pocket and pull them out as they retell the story that Jesus taught about helping:

1) A man was going down a road when robbers attacked him (show the three men).
2) The men beat him and tore his clothes (show the man lying on the ground).
3) A Samaritan came down the road and took care of the injured man (show the Samaritan and the injured man).
4) Jesus told the people He was teaching that they should do the same thing the Samaritan did.

Matthew 7; Luke 10

Jesus Teaches about Helping

Big Book of Bible Story
Coloring Activities for Early Childhood
© David C Cook. Permission granted to photocopy for ministry purposes only.

Matthew 7; Luke 10

Jesus Teaches about Helping

Mary and Martha Follow Jesus

Jesus and Martha Puppets

Supplies

- copy of the Jesus and Martha Puppets (1 per child)
- crayons or washable markers
- scissors
- paper lunch bags (2 per child)
- glue sticks

Directions

Help children color and cut out the Jesus and Martha puppets by cutting around the outside edge and also through the mouth areas as indicated. Help children attach each puppet to a paper lunch bag as shown in the example (glue the top of the face above the fold and the bottom of the face below the fold so that the puppets' mouths open and close). Children can use the puppets to retell the story of Mary and Martha following Jesus from the perspective of either Jesus or Martha. Encourage children to use their imaginations as they play each part.

Luke 10

Mary and Martha Follow Jesus

Jesus Teaches about Praying

Doorknob Prayer Hanger

Supplies

- copy of the Doorknob Prayer Hanger (1 per child)
- crayons or washable markers
- scissors
- glue sticks

Directions

Help children color and cut out the two-sided doorknob hanger. Show the children how to fold the hanger along the dotted line and help them glue the two sides together so the scenes are back-to-back. Children can hang the hangers on the door to their rooms at home as a reminder Jesus taught us when we pray we should go into our rooms and shut the door.

We can pray to God.

Matthew 6; Luke 11

Jesus Teaches about Praying

Jesus Teaches about Sharing

Sharing Placemat

Supplies

- copy of the Sharing Placemat pieces (1 per child)
- construction paper (any color; 1 sheet per child)
- black permanent marker
- crayons or washable markers
- scissors
- pennies (3 per child)
- glue
- clear adhesive covering

Directions

Before class write "I Can Share" at the top of each sheet of construction paper (the paper should be laying horizontally like a placemat when you write these words; see the example).

During class help children color and cut out the three items. Children can draw their favorite foods on the empty plate. They can decorate the shirts to look like their favorite shirts. Help children attach the items to a piece of construction paper with the words "I Can Share" written across the top. Give each child three pennies. Children can attach the pennies to the construction paper around the other items. Use clear adhesive covering over the placemats so they last longer. Children can use the placemats to tell about things they can share with others (food, clothes, toys, and money).

Luke 12

Jesus Teaches about Sharing

Jesus Brings Lazarus Back to Life

Lazarus Lives Flip-Flap Book

Supplies
- copy of the Lazarus Lives Flip-flap book (1 per child)
- crayons or washable markers
- scissors
- construction paper (any color; 1 sheet per child)
- glue sticks

Directions
Help children color and cut out the four scenes. Fold a piece of construction paper in half lengthwise. Cut the top flap of the paper into four equal sections, stopping the cut at the fold line (each flap should be 3" wide). Lift the flaps and glue the scenes under the flaps according to the numbers in each scene. See the small image for an example. Children can use the flip-flap books to retell the story of Jesus bringing Lazarus back to life:

1) Lazarus was sick and he died.
2) Lazarus's sisters were sad and were crying when Jesus came to their house.
3) Jesus went to where Lazarus was buried and told Lazarus to come out.
4) Lazarus came out alive!

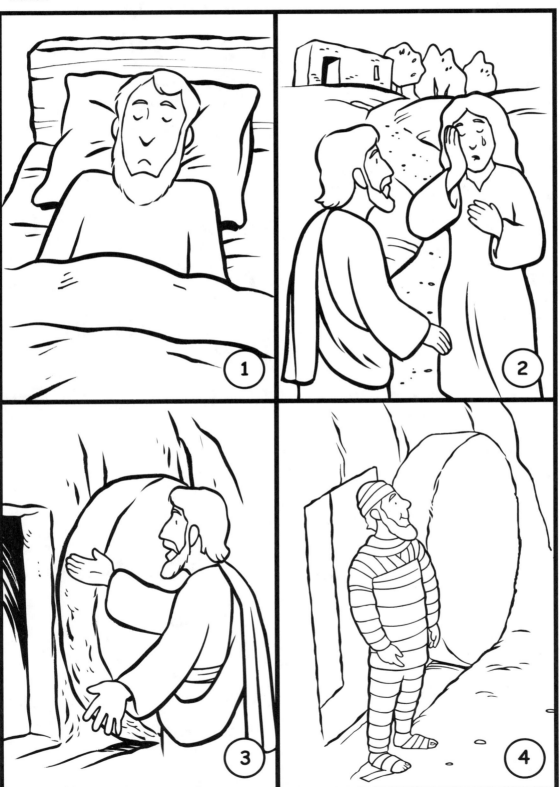

John 11

Jesus Brings Lazarus Back to Life

Jesus Heals Ten Men

Ten Men Finger Puppets

See page 7 for supplies and directions for this activity.

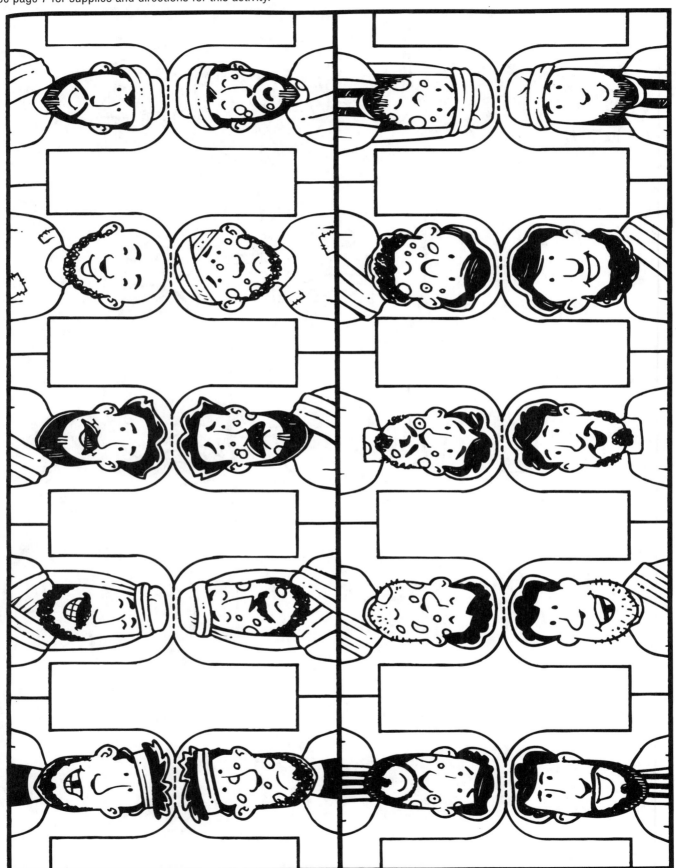

Luke 17

Jesus Heals Ten Men

Jesus and the Children

Jesus and Children Stick Puppets

Supplies

- copy of the Jesus and Children Stick Puppet figures (1 per child)
- crayons or washable markers
- scissors
- tape
- jumbo craft sticks (3 per child)
- clear adhesive covering

Directions

Help children color and cut out the Jesus figure. Cut a slit in the Jesus figure along the bold line above His arms. Children can color the two children figures to look like themselves and a friend (hair color, what they're wearing, etc.). Help children cut out the two children figures. Using tape, children should attach a craft stick to the back of each figure to make three separate stick puppets. Children can slide the puppets of themselves and a friend through the slit above Jesus' arms to look like Jesus is holding them. Kids can use the stick puppets to tell about Jesus spending time with children.

Mark 10

Jesus and the Children

Big Book of Bible Story
Coloring Activities for Early Childhood
© David C Cook. Permission granted to photocopy for ministry purposes only.

Bartimaeus Follows Jesus

Bartimaeus Follows Finger Leg Puppets

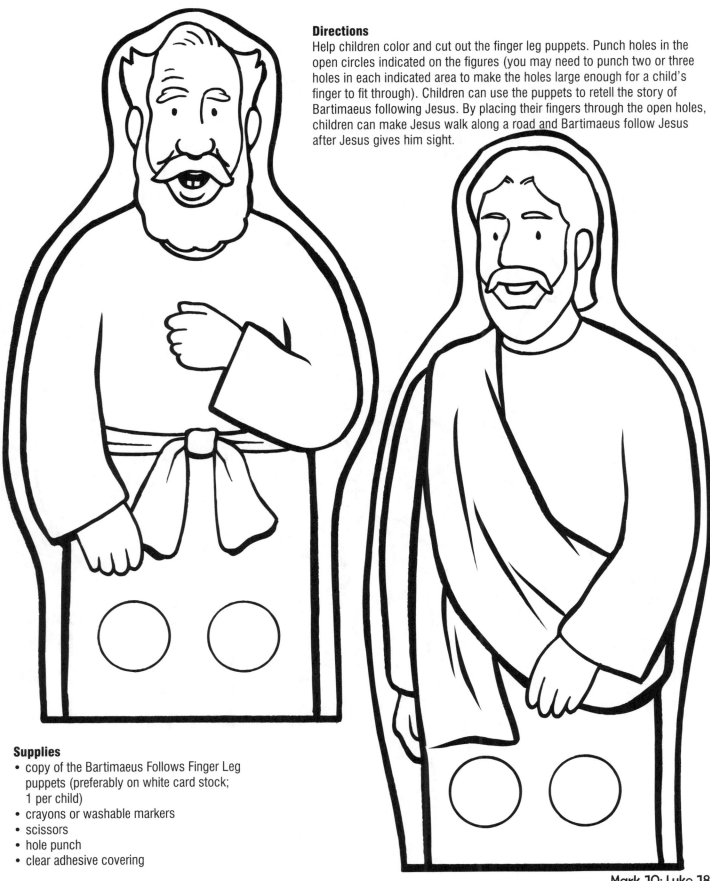

Directions

Help children color and cut out the finger leg puppets. Punch holes in the open circles indicated on the figures (you may need to punch two or three holes in each indicated area to make the holes large enough for a child's finger to fit through). Children can use the puppets to retell the story of Bartimaeus following Jesus. By placing their fingers through the open holes, children can make Jesus walk along a road and Bartimaeus follow Jesus after Jesus gives him sight.

Supplies

- copy of the Bartimaeus Follows Finger Leg puppets (preferably on white card stock; 1 per child)
- crayons or washable markers
- scissors
- hole punch
- clear adhesive covering

Mark 10; Luke 18

Bartimaeus Follows Jesus

Big Book of Bible Story
Coloring Activities for Early Childhood
© David C Cook. Permission granted to photocopy for ministry purposes only.

Jesus and Zacchaeus

Jesus and Zacchaeus Puppets

Supplies

- copy of the Jesus and Zacchaeus puppets (1 per child)
- crayons or washable markers
- scissors
- paper lunch bags (2 per child)
- glue or glue sticks

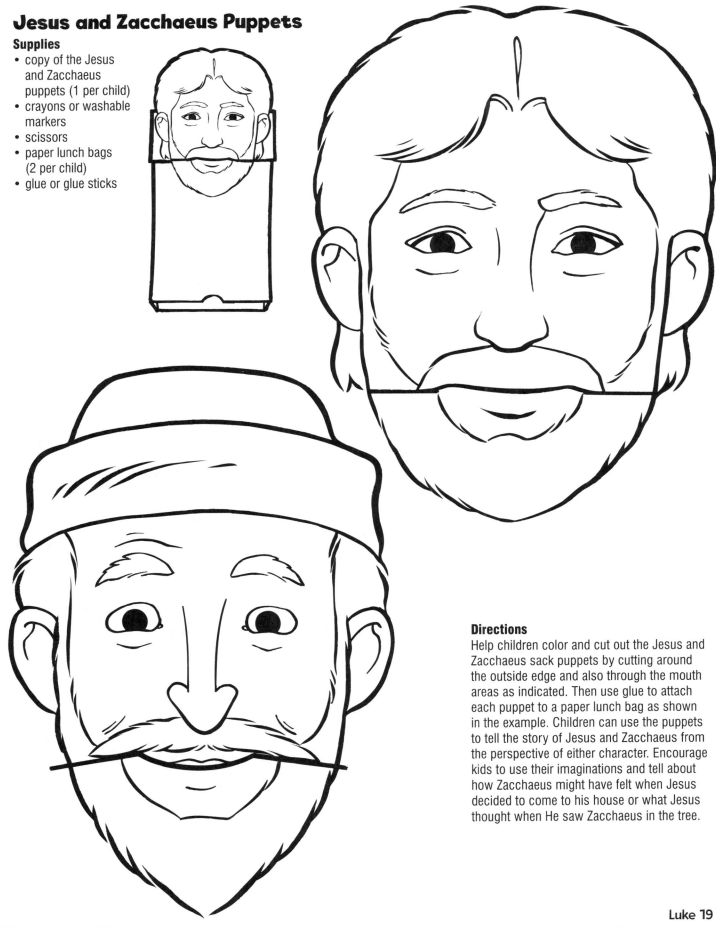

Directions

Help children color and cut out the Jesus and Zacchaeus sack puppets by cutting around the outside edge and also through the mouth areas as indicated. Then use glue to attach each puppet to a paper lunch bag as shown in the example. Children can use the puppets to tell the story of Jesus and Zacchaeus from the perspective of either character. Encourage kids to use their imaginations and tell about how Zacchaeus might have felt when Jesus decided to come to his house or what Jesus thought when He saw Zacchaeus in the tree.

Luke 19

Big Book of Bible Story
Coloring Activities for Early Childhood

Jesus and Zacchaeus

A Crowd Welcomes Jesus

Welcome Puzzle

Supplies

- copy of the Welcome Puzzle (1 per child; preferably on white card stock)
- crayons or washable markers
- scissors

Directions

Help children color and cut out the puzzle pieces. Children can assemble the puzzle to tell about a crowd welcoming Jesus when He rode into Jerusalem.

Matthew 21

A Crowd Welcomes Jesus

People Praise Jesus

Big Book of Bible Story
Coloring Activities for Early Childhood **209**
© David C Cook. Permission granted to photocopy for ministry purposes only.

People Praise Pop-Up Card

Supplies

- copy of the People Praise Pop-Up Card (1 per child)
- crayons or washable markers
- scissors

Directions

Help children color and cut out the People Praise Pop-Up Card (cut only on the solid lines, do not cut on the dotted lines). Show children how to fold the card in half along the horizontal dotted lines so the scenes are back-to-back. Fold the pop-up piece along the dotted line so when the card is opened this piece pops up. Fold the card along the center dotted line so the pop-up piece is folded inside the card (see the example). Children can use the pop-up cards to retell the story of people praising Jesus when He rode into Jerusalem.

Mark 11

People Praise Jesus

Jesus Is Alive!

Tell All Megaphone

Directions

Help children color the three scenes on their megaphones and cut out the megaphones around the outside solid edges. Show children how to roll their megaphones into the proper shape (see the example). Tape the tab under the opposite edge of the megaphone. Children can use the megaphones to tell about Jesus coming back to life:

1) Two women went to Jesus' tomb after He had died.

2) An angel was sitting on the stone that had been rolled away from the tomb's entrance. The angel told the women that Jesus had come back to life.

3) Jesus appeared to the women as they were on their way to tell Jesus' followers what the angel had said.

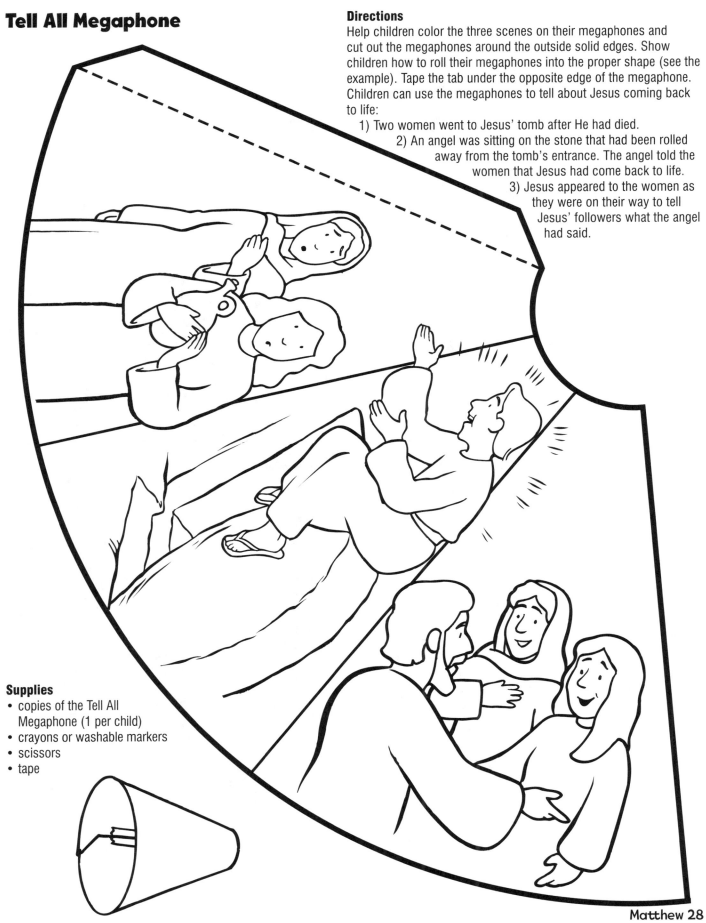

Supplies

- copies of the Tell All Megaphone (1 per child)
- crayons or washable markers
- scissors
- tape

Matthew 28

Jesus Is Alive!

Big Book of Bible Story
Coloring Activities for Early Childhood
© David C Cook. Permission granted to photocopy for ministry purposes only.

Jesus Lives!

Fixin' Fish Flip-Flap Book

Supplies

- copy of the Fixin' Fish Flip-Flap Book scenes (1 per child)
- crayons or washable markers
- scissors
- construction paper (1 sheet per child, any color)
- glue or glue sticks
- various fish stickers *(optional)*

Directions

Before class fold sheets of construction paper in half lengthwise (make one for each child). Cut one half of the paper into three segments by stopping the cut at the fold (see the example).

During class help children color and cut out the three story scenes. Give each child a piece of construction paper that has been prepared ahead of time for the flip-flap book. Show the children how to glue the scenes under the flaps (see the example). Children can lift each flap as they retell the story of Jesus appearing alive to His followers.

Optional: Allow children to attach fish stickers to the front of each flap as a reminder that Jesus helped His followers catch fish when He appeared to them.

John 21

Jesus Lives!

Peter Preaches about Jesus

Peter's Megaphone

Directions
Help children color and cut out the megaphone (cut only around the outside outline, do not cut apart the individual scenes). Assist the children as they roll their megaphones into a cone shape. Tape along the seam. Children can use the megaphone to tell about the early church. They can also use the megaphone as they pretend to be Peter speaking on the day of Pentecost.

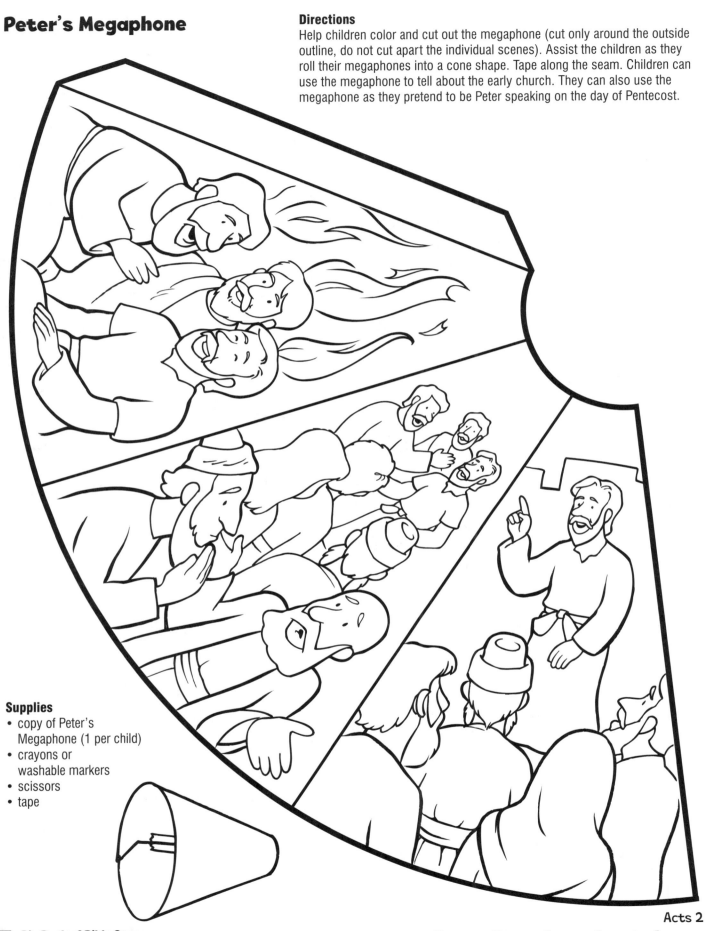

Supplies
- copy of Peter's Megaphone (1 per child)
- crayons or washable markers
- scissors
- tape

Acts 2

Peter Preaches about Jesus

The Church Follows Jesus

Church Storybook

Supplies

- copy of the Church Storybook scenes and word strips (1 per child; continued on p. 219)
- crayons or washable markers
- scissors
- construction paper (any color, 1 sheet per child)
- glue sticks
- hole punch
- yarn (any color)

Directions

Before class, cut one piece of construction paper into four equal sections for each child in your class.

During class help children color and cut out each scene and word strip. Help children glue the scenes in order on the precut rectangles of construction paper. The title cover should be on its own piece. Scenes 1 and 2 should be back-to-back on a second piece, and scenes 3 and 4 should be back-to-back on a third piece. The last rectangle of construction paper can be used as a back for the book. Under each scene the children should glue the matching word strip. Help children place all of their construction paper rectangles in order (like a book) according to the numbers in the lower corners of each scene. Punch holes along one side or along the top of the pages of the book and tie the book together using yarn. Children can use their books to tell about the church following Jesus:

1) The church gathered to break bread together in their homes.
2) They prayed together.
3) They met together at the temple every day.
4) They gave their money to help others.

The believers broke bread together in their homes.

The believers prayed together.

The believers met together at the temple every day.

The believers gave their money to help others.

Acts 2, 4

The Church Follows Jesus

Big Book of Bible Story
Coloring Activities for Early Childhood
© David C Cook. Permission granted to photocopy for ministry purposes only.

Peter and John at the Temple

Healed Man Matching Game

Supplies

- 2 copies of Healed Man Matching Game for each child
- crayons or washable markers
- scissors

Directions

Help children color and cut out two sets of the Healed Man Matching Game cards. Children should color each set of cards to look exactly alike. Show children how to use the cards to play a matching game. Mix up all ten cards and place them all facedown on the floor or on a table. Children can turn over one card and then guess which card to turn over next to find its match. If they are successful in finding a matching pair of cards, they may keep the cards. If they do not find a match, they should turn both cards back over (facing down) and try again on their next turn. Once the children have made all five matches, they can place the cards in order per the numbers in the lower right corner and use the cards to retell the story of Peter and John at the temple:

1) Peter and John went to the temple.
2) They came to the temple gate called Beautiful.
3) They saw a man who had been crippled all his life. He was asking for money.
4) Peter told the man to stand up and walk by the power of Jesus Christ. The man jumped up and began to walk.
5) The people were amazed.

Acts 3

Peter and John at the Temple

Big Book of Bible Story
Coloring Activities for Early Childhood
© David C Cook. Permission granted to photocopy for ministry purposes only.

Philip Tells about Jesus

Philip Tells Triangle

Supplies

- copy of Philip Tells Triangle (1 per child)
- crayons or washable markers
- scissors
- tape

Directions

Help children color cut out the Philip Tells Triangle around the outside edge (do not cut on the dotted lines). Show the children how to fold the triangle on the dotted lines to form the finished shape (see the example). Tape the tab on scene 3 to the back of scene 1 to finish the activity. Children can use the triangle to retell the story of Philip telling the Ethiopian man about Jesus.

Acts 8

Philip Tells about Jesus

Saul Begins to Follow Jesus

Saul Story Wheel

Supplies

- copy of the Saul Story Wheel (1 per child)
- copy of the story wheel cover on p. 106 (1 per child)
- crayons or washable markers
- scissors
- hole punch
- paper fasteners (1 per child)

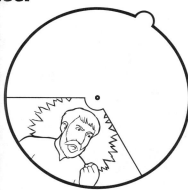

Directions

Help children color and cut out the story wheel and cover. Punch a hole through the center of both the cover and the wheel where it is indicated by the open circle. Attach the cover over the wheel using a paper fastener. Children can turn the wheels and look through the openings as they retell the story of Saul beginning to follow Jesus:

1) Saul did not like Jesus' followers. He was mean to them and tried to arrest them.
2) On his way to a city to search for followers of Jesus, a bright light flashed and Saul heard Jesus speaking to him. Saul could not see and Jesus told him to go into the city.
3) The Lord told a man named Ananias to go to Saul. Ananias went to Saul and Saul was able to see. Saul got up and was baptized. He followed Jesus.

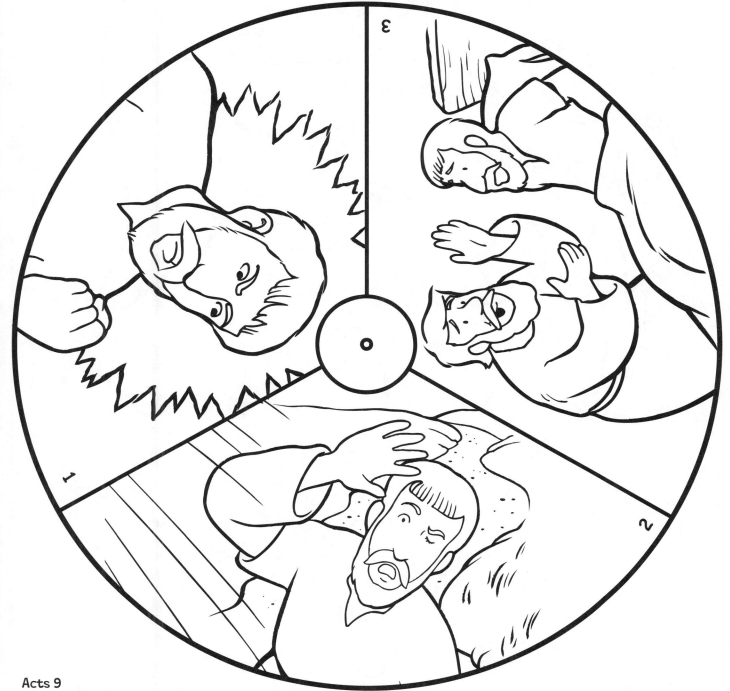

Acts 9

Saul Begins to Follow Jesus

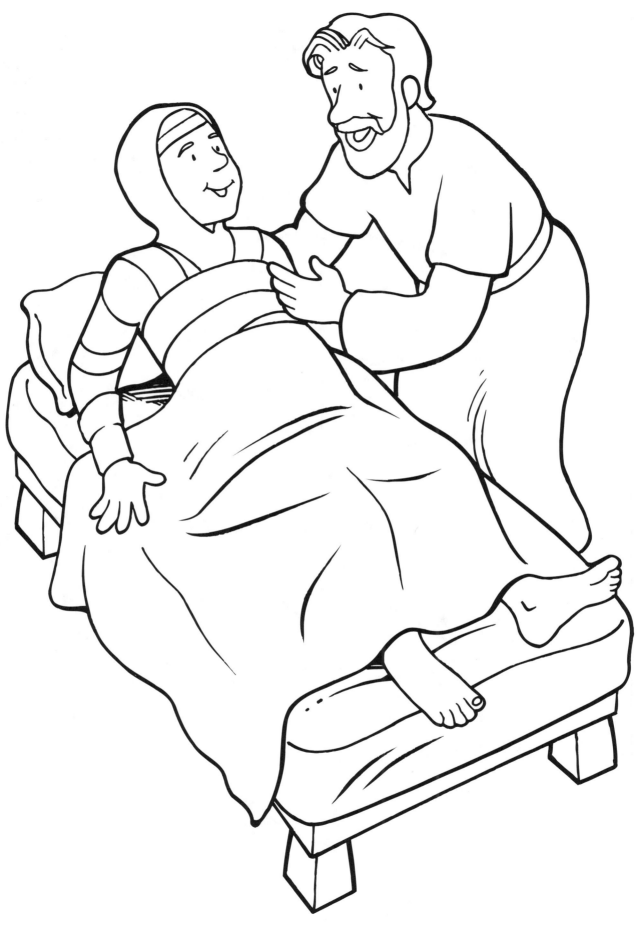

Big Book of Bible Story
Coloring Activities for Early Childhood
© David C Cook. Permission granted to photocopy for ministry purposes only.

Peter and Tabitha

Peter and Tabitha Hand Puppets

Supplies

- copy of the Peter and Tabitha Hand Puppets (1 per child)
- crayons or washable markers
- scissors
- tape

Directions

Help children color and cut out the two hand puppets. Show the children how to fold the puppets in half on the dotted lines and tape the sides together so each puppet fits on the child's hand like a mitten. Assist each child in putting the Peter puppet on one hand and the Tabitha puppet on the other hand. Children can use the puppets to retell the story of Peter raising Tabitha from the dead from the perspective of Peter and Tabitha. Children can tell about how Peter might have felt when he saw Tabitha's sad friends and what he might have said when he knelt and prayed. Children can also tell about how Tabitha might have felt when Peter helped her up out of bed and how happy she might have been to see her friends again.

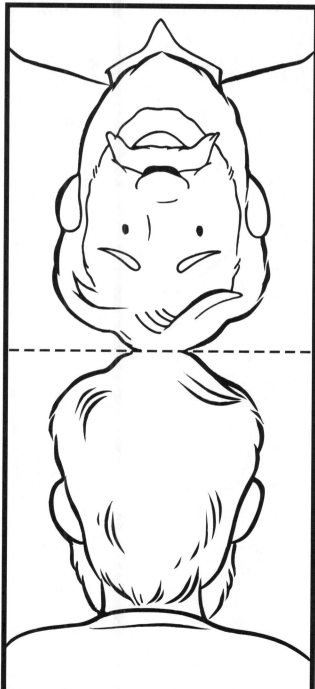

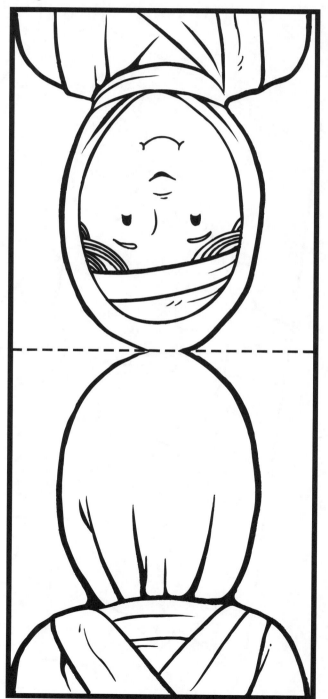

Acts 9

Peter and Tabitha

The Church Prays for Peter in Prison

Praying for Peter Storybook

Supplies

- copy of the Praying for Peter Storybook cover and story strips (1 per child; continued on p. 230)
- crayons or washable markers
- scissors
- construction paper (light color, 5 sheets per child)
- glue or glue sticks
- 3-hole punch
- yarn (any color)

Directions

Help children color cover and story strips. pieces of light colored paper. Help children attach one piece of construction the cover aside. On the of construction paper, help draw bars to resemble a and attach the first word the bottom of this page. third piece of construction help children trace one of their hands as a reminder that the church prayed for Peter in prison. Help the children attach the second word strip at the bottom of this page. On the fourth piece of construction paper children should draw an angel and attach the third word strip at the bottom of this page. On the last piece of paper, children should draw a house with a door as a reminder that Peter went to the house of the believers and knocked on the door. Help the children attach the last word strip at the bottom of this page. Put the pages in order (according to the numbers on the word strips) and place the cover on the front. Punch holes along the left side of the book and use yarn to tie the book together. Children can use their books to retell the story of Peter in prison and the church praying for him.

1 — Peter was in jail.

2 — The church prayed for Peter.

3 — An angel led Peter out of jail.

4 — Peter went to a house to see the believers.

Acts 12

The Church Prays for Peter in Prison

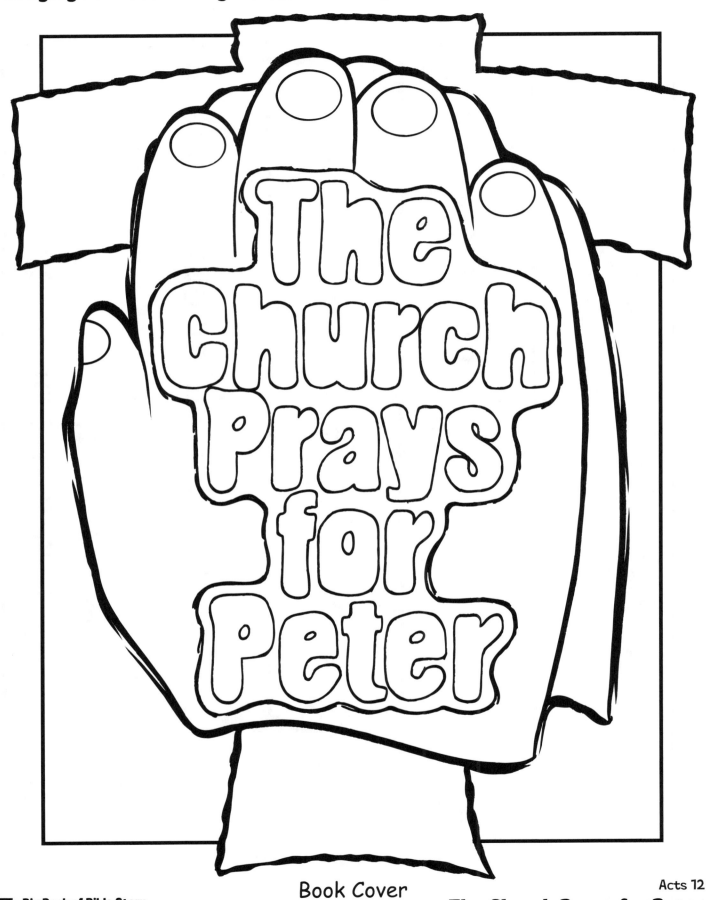

Book Cover

Acts 12

The Church Prays for Peter

Lydia Follows Jesus

Lydia Follows Story Pamphlet

Supplies

- copy of the Lydia Follows Story Pamphlet (1 per child)
- crayons or washable markers
- scissors

Directions

Help children color and cut out the Lydia Follows Story Pamphlet. Show children how to fold the pamphlet along the dotted lines. Fold the pamphlet in half lengthwise along the long dotted line so the scenes are back-to-back (three scenes on each side). Lay the pamphlet down so scene 3 is in front of you. Fold in scene 2. Fold in scene 1 so it becomes the cover of the pamphlet (see the example). Children can use the pamphlets to retell the story of Lydia following Jesus.

Step 1

Step 2

Step 3

Acts 16

Lydia Follows Jesus

The Jailer Follows Jesus

Jailer's Sword and Shield Scenes

Supplies

- copy of the Jailer's Sword and Shield Scenes pieces for each child (1 per child; preferably on card stock)
- crayons or washable markers
- scissors
- hole punch
- paper fasteners (1 per child
- clear adhesive covering

Directions

Help children color and cut out the sword and shield pieces (leave the shield in one piece, do not cut apart the individual scenes). Punch a hole in the center of the shield and through the end of the sword where indicated by the open circle. Attach the sword to the shield using a paper fastener (see the example). Children can spin their swords and when they land on a scene, children can retell that part of the story of the jailer following Jesus:

1) Paul and Silas were in jail.
2) Paul and Silas chose to sing songs to God even though they were in jail.
3) Suddenly, there was an earthquake and the doors broke open and Paul's and Silas's chains fell off. The jailer was afraid that the prisoners had escaped so he was going to hurt himself.
4) Paul and Silas told the jailer about Jesus and the jailer and his family were baptized that night.

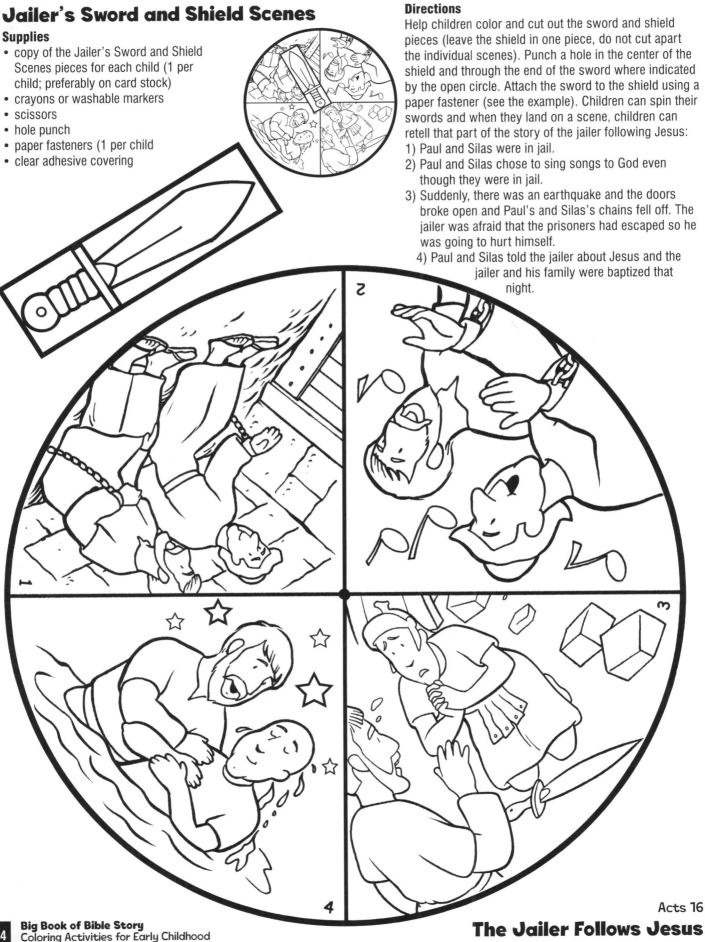

Acts 16

The Jailer Follows Jesus

Paul Helps People Follow Jesus

Paul Mask

Supplies

- copy of the Paul Mask (1 per child)
- crayons or washable markers
- scissors
- jumbo craft sticks
  (1 per child)
- tape

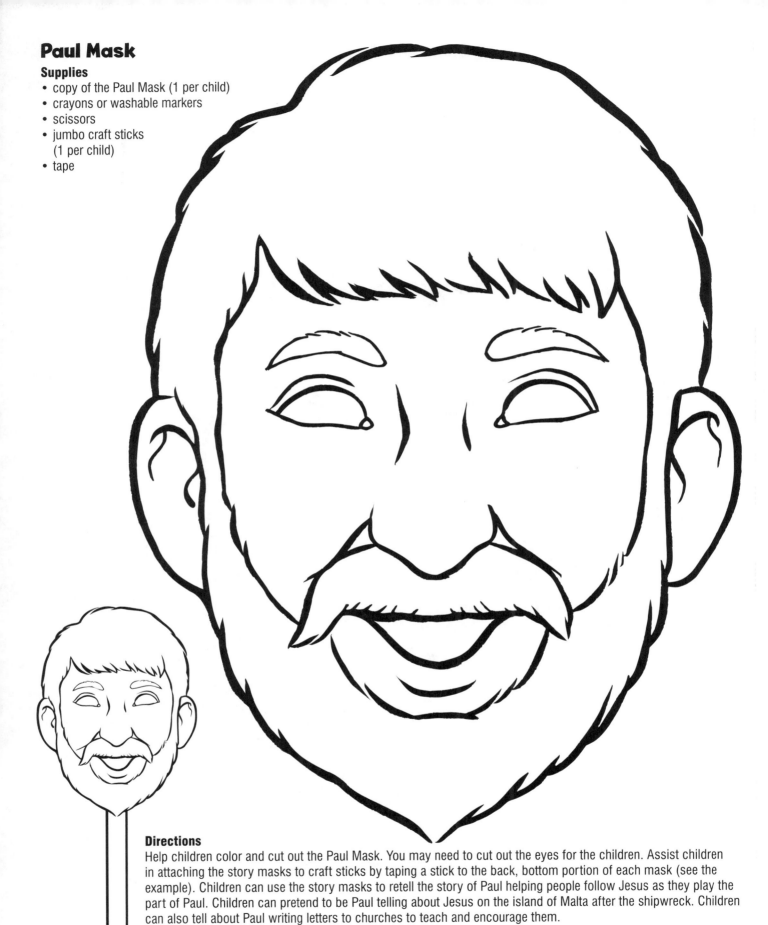

Directions

Help children color and cut out the Paul Mask. You may need to cut out the eyes for the children. Assist children in attaching the story masks to craft sticks by taping a stick to the back, bottom portion of each mask (see the example). Children can use the story masks to retell the story of Paul helping people follow Jesus as they play the part of Paul. Children can pretend to be Paul telling about Jesus on the island of Malta after the shipwreck. Children can also tell about Paul writing letters to churches to teach and encourage them.

Acts 28; Ephesians 4, 6; Philippians 1–2; Colossians 4

Paul Helps People Follow Jesus

Big Book of Bible Story
Coloring Activities for Early Childhood
© David C Cook. Permission granted to photocopy for ministry purposes only.

Preschool/Pre-K & K Scope & Sequence

Fall Year 1
- God Made the Sky and Earth (pp. 8–9)
- God Made Fish and Birds (pp. 10–11)
- God Made Animals (pp. 12–14)
- God Made People (pp. 17–19)
- Noah Builds a Boat (pp. 29–30)
- Noah and the Flood (pp. 31–32)
- Abram Moves (pp. 33–34)
- Abram and Lot (pp. 35–36)
- Abraham and Sarah Have a Baby (pp. 37–38)
- Joseph as a Boy (pp. 39–40)
- Joseph Serves God All His Life (pp. 41–42)
- Samuel as a Boy (pp. 65–66)
- Samuel Serves God All His Life (pp. 67–69)

Winter Year 1
- An Angel Announces Jesus' Birth (pp. 125–126)
- Jesus Is Born (pp. 129–131)
- Shepherds Visit Jesus (pp. 136–137)
- Simeon and Anna See Jesus (pp. 138–139)
- Wise Men Worship Jesus (pp. 143–144)
- Jesus as a Boy (pp. 145–146)
- Jesus Is Baptized (pp. 147–148)
- Jesus Is Tempted (pp. 149–150)
- Jesus Begins to Teach (pp. 158–160)
- Jesus and the Children (pp. 201–202)
- Jesus and Matthew (pp. 165–166)
- Jesus and a Woman from Samaria (pp. 153–155)
- Jesus and Zacchaeus (pp. 205–206)

Spring Year 1
- Triumphal Entry: People Praise Jesus (pp. 209–210)
- Resurrection Sunday: Jesus Lives! (pp. 213–214)
- Jesus Heals an Official's Son (pp. 156–157)
- Jesus Heals a Man Who Could Not Walk (pp. 163–164)
- Jesus Heals the Soldier's Servant (pp. 171–172)
- Jesus Brings a Young Man Back to Life (pp. 173–174)
- Jesus Walks on Water (pp. 181–183)
- Jesus Heals a Man Who Could Not Hear or Speak (pp. 184–185)
- Peter Preaches about Jesus (pp. 215–216)
- Peter and John at the Temple (pp. 220–221)
- Philip Tells about Jesus (pp. 222–223)
- Peter and Tabitha (pp. 226–227)
- The Church Prays for Peter in Prison (pp. 228–230)

Summer Year 1
- David Plays for Saul (pp. 70–72)
- David Meets Goliath (pp. 73–74)
- David and Jonathan (pp. 75–76)
- David and Mephibosheth (pp. 77–78)
- David Sings to God (pp. 79–80)
- Solomon Prays to Know What Is Right (pp. 81–82)
- Solomon Builds the Temple (pp. 83–85)
- Jehoshaphat Asks for God's Help (pp. 107–108)
- Josiah Reads God's Word (pp. 104–106)
- Elisha and a Widow's Oil (pp. 95–97)
- Elisha and a Shunammite Family (pp. 98–99)
- Elisha and the Shunammite's Son (pp. 100–101)
- Elisha and Naaman (pp. 102–103)

Fall Year 2

- God Made a World for People (pp. 15–16)
- God Made Adam and Eve (pp. 20–22)
- God Made My Senses (pp. 23–25)
- God Made Me Special (pp. 26–28)
- Moses Is Born (pp. 43–44)
- Moses Leads God's People (pp. 45–46)
- God's People Cross the Red Sea (pp. 47–48)
- God Provides for His People (pp. 49–50)
- God Gives Ten Rules (pp. 51–52)
- Joshua and Caleb (pp. 53–54)
- God's People Cross the Jordan River (pp. 55–56)
- The Fall of Jericho (pp. 57–58)
- Joshua Talks to God's People (pp. 59–60)

Winter Year 2

- An Angel Brings Special News (pp. 127–128)
- A Special Baby Is Born (pp. 132–133)
- Shepherds Hear Special News (pp. 134–135)
- Wise Men Worship a Special Baby (pp. 140–142)
- Jesus Teaches about Pleasing God (pp. 167–168)
- Jesus Teaches about Giving (pp. 169–170)
- Jesus Teaches about Praying (pp. 193–194)
- Jesus Teaches about Helping (pp. 188–190)
- Jesus Teaches about Sharing (pp. 195–196)
- Two Friends Follow Jesus (pp. 151–152)
- Fishermen Follow Jesus (pp. 161–162)
- Mary and Martha Follow Jesus (pp. 191–192)
- Bartimaeus Follows Jesus (pp. 203–204)

Spring Year 2

- Triumphal Entry: A Crowd Welcomes Jesus (pp. 207–208)
- Resurrection Sunday: Jesus Is Alive! (pp. 211–212)
- Jesus Stops a Storm (pp. 175–176)
- Jesus Heals a Young Girl (pp. 177–178)
- Jesus Feeds a Crowd (pp. 179–180)
- Jesus Heals a Man Born Blind (pp. 186–187)
- Jesus Heals Ten Men (pp. 199–200)
- Jesus Brings Lazarus Back to Life (pp. 197–198)
- The Church Follows Jesus (pp. 217–219)
- Saul Begins to Follow Jesus (pp. 224–225)
- Lydia Follows Jesus (pp. 231–232)
- The Jailer Follows Jesus (pp. 233–234)
- Paul Helps People Follow Jesus (pp. 235–236)

Summer Year 2

- Elijah Is Fed by Ravens (pp. 86–88)
- Elijah Helps a Widow (pp. 89–90)
- Elijah Helps a Widow's Son (pp. 91–92)
- Elijah and the Prophets of Baal (pp. 93–94)
- Daniel and His Friends Obey God (pp. 114–115)
- Daniel's Friends Worship Only God (pp. 116–117)
- Daniel and the Handwriting on the Wall (pp. 118–119)
- Daniel and the Lions' Den (pp. 120–121)
- Gideon Leads God's Army (pp. 61–62)
- Ruth Makes Good Choices (pp. 63–64)
- Jonah Tells about God (pp. 122–124)
- Esther Helps God's People (pp. 112–113)
- Nehemiah Rebuilds the Wall (pp. 109–111)